A brief account of two years in a little house
in the medina of Marrakesh
2006-8

Note to the reader

I once wrote a book about the love lives of some rather ordinary young women and a most eminent critic, hoping for something entirely different - and wittier - in the manner of Fairbanks and Waugh, complained that it was a domestic comedy. So I'd better explain what this little book is not - not a history of Morocco, nor a treatise on American or Middle Eastern politics or even the position of women in Islam, it isn't even even a how-to book extolling the virtues of Moroccan design. These are things quite beyond my comprehension and much better dealt with elsewhere. It is merely the account of two years living in the medina of Marrakesh - rather heavy on cats and food and the trivia of everyday life and has no message or moral at all.

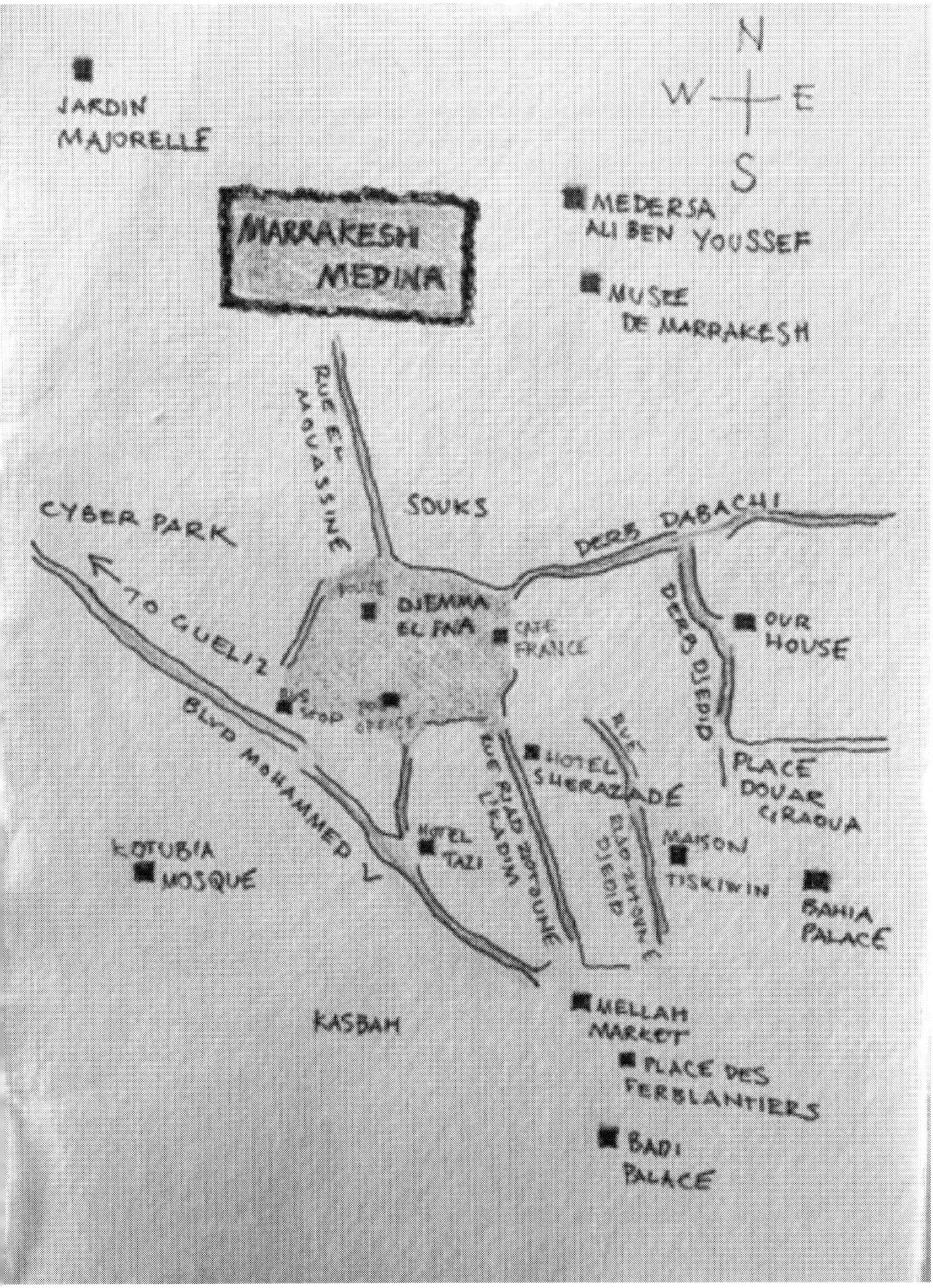
N
W
E
S
JARDIN MAJORELLE
MARRAKESH MEDINA
MEDERSA ALI BEN YOUSSEF
MUSEE DE MARRAKESH
RUE EL MOUASSINE
SOUKS
CYBER PARK
DERB DABACHI
TO GUELIZ
DJEMMA EL FNA
CAFE FRANCE
OUR HOUSE
DERB DJEDID
STOP
OFFICE
BLVD MOHAMMED V
RUE RIAD ZITOUNE EL KADIM
HOTEL SHERAZADE
RUE RIAD ZITOUNE DJEDID
PLACE DOUAR GRAOUA
HOTEL TAZI
MAISON TISKIWIN
KOTUBIA MOSQUE
BAHIA PALACE
MELLAH MARKET
KASBAH
PLACE DES FERBLANTIERS
BADI PALACE

Glossary

dar - house
derb - an alley or lane
djedid - new
Djemma ElFna - the big square in Marrakesh
Gueliz - the new part of town
hanut - little local shop
medina - the old part of town
riad - traditional house with a courtyard sometimes containing fruit trees

The Beginning

In 2006 we bought a five hundred year old mud brick house in Marrakesh, in an alley off derb Dabachi, five minutes walk from Djemma Elfna where snake charmers prod unenthusiastic cobras, men with shell-encrusted beanies twirl their heads all day, and drummers drum without ceasing. You can buy elixirs for whatever ails you from men whose shops consist of three square foot of carpet, and water from the leather pouches of Berbers wearing hats decorated with pink and yellow bobbles. Your teeth can be pulled en plein air by not-necessarily-very-clean pliers.

You can buy wooden snakes and orange and pink kites which break even before you get them home, and dates and dried figs and have orange juice squeezed in front of your eyes.

It was madness, of course, to leave the comforts of Manhattan, with its subways, dishwashers and decent pizza, for a place where donkey carts, mopeds and abject beggars clutter the streets. But it was romantic. No question about that. Different and sometimes bizarre. We liked that at first.

It all began long before. My husband and I met in Florence in the early 70's where each of us had gone to live untrammeled, bohemian lives as painters far away from our pleasant, dull, families. Between then and 2006 all sorts of things happened. We brought up two children, who, in due course of time, left home. The cat lived to be eighteen and the dog to the eve of his sixteenth birthday. Then that era was over.

Meanwhile Italy became prosperous and expensive. George Bush rendered the United States fascist and unpleasant. England remained damp and Florida wasn't really a place we had any desire to live.

For some years we had been spending spring breaks in Morocco and both of us had fallen head over heels for the exoticism, the sun, the date palms hugging the rivers in the south, the snowcapped Atlas mountains, the unpronounceable language - the whole shebang in fact.

On chilly February days we would pore over the internet real estate listings of desirable dars and ravishing riads and would feast on dreams of escape.

We decided, in the end, that renting for six months would be a good idea. We would dip our toes into Morocco and see what happened next.

It was May and beautifully sunny on the roof of Hotel Sherazade in the heart of the medina. Surrounded by potted palms and hibiscus, bougainvillea and pomegranates, we sipped mint tea and plotted. Our daughter, escaped from the gloom of London, was tanning her pallid legs.

I can't remember exactly why we were in the new part of town the next day - probably something to do with getting Claudia the sort of croissant she likes. Anyway, she saw Amagusta Agence Immobilier on the corner of the Mohammed V and Boulevard Zerktouni. We studied the pictures of riads in the glass showcases. They all looked quite wonderful.

"Well, you should at least go in and ask," Claudia said. "Isn't that what you're here for, old people?"

So we walked up two flights of concrete stairs and entered an office where I tried to explain to the secretary, in my defective French, that we'd like to rent a house in Marrakech for six months.

Enter Henri Marchive the owner of the business, a middle-aged Frenchman equipped with a cell phone. His English was quite as bad as my French. I tried to explain that we wanted to rent something old and charming, but probably not derelict, because what would happen if it fell down? M. Marchive thought the renting idea seemed to be a bit complicated; it was easy to get a vacation rental for rent for a week or a month - but six months? We might as well buy something.

Yes, but we didn't really have that much money. It would have to be rather a modest place - a very modest place. The smallest place that possibly was. But of course there would be no harm in looking...

Out in the bright sunlight of the street, I said to Robert, "I thought we were only looking to rent somewhere."

"We are, but you never know."

We went to two other agencies and made appointments with them too. Then we returned to the hotel in the medina where Claudia retreated to bed since her stomach was still bad. The croissant hadn't done the trick.

In the late afternoon, Robert and I went to the Cafe France on the north side of Djemma elFna, that circus of snake charmers, potion sellers and henna ladies, and sat on little chairs under the red awning and waited to see if Henri Marchive would turn up. I thought he wouldn't, or else be hours late, because this was Morocco where time seemed more fluid than in New York. Robert ordered a mineral water and I had *the* Lipton and we watched the world go by and waited for the little boy who sold fresh macaroons from a tray. The whole world did go by: tourists wearing all sorts of unsuitable skimpy clothing and men in jellabas and one in a fez. Most of the Moroccan women were modestly dressed and wore headscarves. One or two had accessorized their outfits with running shoes and a baseball hats. Shoe shine men tapped their boxes and sellers of phone cards clicked them. A stream of mopeds, bicycles, donkey carts and caleches passed by, but no cars since they are banned in the square in the afternoon.

"Are we quite mad?" Robert said.

"I haven't the least idea. Perhaps Henri Marchive will never arrive and we won't have to worry about it." I ordered another glass of tea.

At 4:02 precisely, Henri M. arrived riding pillion on the back of a motor scooter driven by one of his assistants. And so we set off, as briskly as the milling crowds permitted, north up rue Dabachi. We passed through an archway lined by clothing shops and along a road crowded cluttered with cake, toy and fruit stalls. We passed a clock repair shop and a laundry. Then a small mosque, a pharmacy and more clothes shops where the battered, kaftan-wearing mannequins had bland expressions and looked as if they came from the 1950's. There was a wood shop too and lots of places to buy spices.

After the flashing neon eyeglasses of *Optique Dabachi*, we turned right onto Derb Djedid which sloped slightly downward and was much quieter. A few cats loitered and some children played, but the alley too medieval and narrow for anything wider than a handcart. Directly facing us was a tiny shop, no bigger than a large closet, selling bread and jelly and OMO and penny candies. "Bis 23" was written above it in wavering painted letters. Then another corner and a dark brown door, with a hand of Fatima knocker, set in the thick walls.

Henri Marchive knocked, the door opened and we stepped down out of the 21st century into the hall of the smallest riad in the world. The floor was pink and green tile and the walls were bright lemon yellow above tobacco-colored tadelakt. An Ali Baba archway joined the hall with a miniature courtyard which was open to the sky.

Off the courtyard there was a small salon with red hand-painted doors, and a fireplace, cut plasterwork and little plinths that might have shown off awards. There was a bed room too with a hammered copper wash basin. The minute kitchen was mostly taken up by an an ancient American size refrigerator.

On the next floor there were two more bedrooms. An uneven tiled staircase led to the roof terrace from which you could see the snow-topped Atlas Mountains in one direction beyond the crenellated facade of an old lycee. If we turned south we could see the tower of the Kotubia. A thin, sad olive tree eked out its existence in a huge terra cotta pot. We were warned not to look north over the wall behind the washing line: a very religious family lived next door and would be upset if we saw them.

"A pity Claudia didn't come with us," I said.

Robert took photos of all the rooms.

Then we walked with Henri Marchive to another riad which was much bigger - the terrace was on two levels. In the main part of the house a group of young people giggled on a sofa, probably hiding from their parents. There were cracks in the plaster work and we weren't interested in this one at all - besides which there were six bedrooms. It was too tall and gloomy altogether. It wasn't a bit like the little house on derb Djedid.

By supper time Claudia was somewhat recovered.

"You should have come with us," I said. "We saw the most exquisite little house. It was five hundred years old."

"Then buy it," Claudia said.

"Fine for you to say. Since you're not actually paying for it."

"Yes, but I'd come and stay in it."

"I bet you would."

You cannot possibly buy the very first house you see, so we kept our appointment with another real estate agency. A young man picked us up by the French consulate exactly when he said he would. The three of us crammed into a tiny Fiat and sped off into the medina, down the narrow, crowded streets scattering donkeys and old ladies left and right. I kept my eyes shut, not wanting to see whatever disasters we might have caused. I wasn't even sure if we were allowed to take a car through such narrow lanes. The young man from the real estate agency wasn't very chatty - he was too busy almost killing people.

The riad he eventually showed us was too big, needed too much work and was too near the city wall. It was a family home, and all the family were there including their twenty-something Down's syndrome daughter who sat surrounded by toys on a rug in the courtyard and smiled beatifically at us too. Her mother had dressed her up so prettily with pink and purple barrettes in her hair. I wondered if the family dreaded being displaced by rich, careless foreigners or whether they needed the money for their daughter's care. But we knew immediately that it wasn't going to be us.

What the nameless young man showed us next was quite hopeless - outside the medina, in a brand new development. We might just as well be in Florida. "You don't want to see the swimming pool?" he asked.

"No, it won't be necessary."

Realizing that we were a dead loss, he sped off towards the Ville Nouvelle screaming furiously into his cell phone and ignoring us.

Of course, we had fallen madly in love with the very first house, the little house that was a bis - a house chopped in two - so we set about buying it. This sounds very simple, but it wasn't. We had seen a grand total of four houses - three really since the last one was a condo.

We returned to the cold, late spring of New York full of visions of warmth, telephoned Henri Marchive and told him that as soon as we had got the money together we would send it to the notary who was handling the deal. And no, we did not want the contents of the house - not the blue velvet banquettes nor the twirly wrought iron bedsteads, or the skin lanterns with henna designs on, or even the alarming vast refrigerator. We were quite capable of buying our own furniture and were not about to pay several thousand euros for some one else's dream of Marrakshi delights.

In Morocco, where most transactions are done in cash in order to escape the outstretched hand of the tax man, there are two payments. Put rather simply: there is the actual price of the property and the declared one. The over the table and under the table.

We sent a Swift transfer for all sorts on money off into the ether - Robert said we could have just thrown the check out of the window. In late August we set out from New York.

The thought of carting six months' worth of stuff down the subway stairs, changing at Penn Station and then again at Jamaica was daunting, so we opted for a limo. Alex from the Ukraine made a U-turn on 23rd Street and sped off furiously to the airport. Robert thought he would kill us; I merely thought since I was going on an aeroplane and likely to die anyway it didn't much matter. A driver in Queens leant out of his window and yelled "Fucking asshole" at Alex which we thought fair. Alex spent most of the trip on his cell phone arguing with the dispatcher about his next fare - but turned to us with a wide grin and assured us we had got "the right driver". We were afraid not to tip him because he was so very large and angry.

The flight to Casablanca was thankfully unremarkable. We changed at Casablanca and caught the short flight to Marrakech where we discovered that our luggage had vanished. The desk clerk, only too used to the task, took notes on the sizes and colors of our suitcases. Then, unburdened by baggage, we took the bus into town.

Everyone was very pleased to see us at Hotel Sherazade where our room was on the ground floor. There was an enormous bed and a very basic private bathroom and, blessing indeed, a fan. It was astoundingly hot - over 100F in the afternoon when we went back to the airport to look for our luggage, found it, and returned with it. Back at Sherazade I discovered that I still didn't have the little red bag- and went back again on my own and got it. Arrived at last.

In the evening we had a drink in Cafe France and then, unable to contain our eagerness, went and stood outside the little house on derb Djedid. When I peeped in through the letter box, all I saw was the skinny arm of the young man who was looking after the house. We felt embarrassed and left. All we wanted was for all the paperwork to be over and our adventure to begin.

The next morning it was still astoundingly hot. After orange juice and baguettes on Sherazade's roof we took the bus up to the Ville Nouvelle. M. Marchive had just got back that morning from the long French August holiday and said everything was in order. The closing was to be on September 8th. In preparation Robert opened a bank account at BMCI where there was more air-conditioning - bliss. Only ten more days.

In the afternoon I ventured out to a cramped internet place where teenagers sat four to a computer playing games and all of the much-used machines had blurred letters or none. The keyboard is set out differently than a US or English one so I spent a lot of time stabbing randomly and hoping my emails made some sort of sense. The little children running the place laughed at my efforts.

The days waiting to move in to the little house were spent first at Sherazade and then at Dar Limoune (Orange House) where our room was painted a soft cream and the doors were green. The whole place had been recently renovated and there was a beautiful fragile looking jasmine in the courtyard.

One evening when we were sitting on the top terrace after dinner, we were joined by a plump American, his glamorous Romanian wife and their little daughter, Isabella. This was the first American family we had encountered. John was on holiday from the American Foreign Service in Mauritania and reported to the State Department. They described picnics in the desert where they sat surrounded by armed guards. We did not quite know what to make of this, and did not want to discuss American foreign policy so steered clear of politics entirely.

Going out for dinner should be a treat, not something which you do everyday when it stops being a treat. Going out for dinner for two weeks straight is torture.

At The Terraces of the Alhambra we had a dried-up pizza. At the eccentric Dar Mimoune, with its huge, fruit tree-filled courtyard where cats and guinea fowl roam and the staff endlessly squabble, we ate excellent lamb brochettes and the best *salad marocaine*.

We ended up eating most often at Premices a new restaurant right on the corner of Djemma el Fna and rue riad Zitoune l'Kadim. It isn't a bit expensive. Menu: couscous and seven vegetables, brochettes, omelets, pizzas, fries, salad nicoise, good deserts like mille feuille, creme brulee and ice cream which is more like sorbet. The salads have a slightly bleach-like taste. From their terrace you can see the orange sellers' carts, a rug shop, a mosque, two other restaurants, and, further off, the huge open air barbecue that the whole square becomes at night. And lots and lots of people trudging around.

The second evening we were there we noticed a square little boy of about eighteen months running between the mosque and the orange carts. His round head and his body shape and movements were exactly like our son's at that age. The way he would raise his arms or bend forward from the waist were identical. He was always very busy talking to other children or pushing old people in wheelchairs or going up to random people in the other restaurants or running to the orange stand.

He was a delight to watch - the only thing was that this was a public square with mopeds and the occasional car going through - not to mention all sorts of people some of whom probably aren't nice at all. We eventually worked out that the boy's inattentive mother was sitting next to the mosque. One evening the short chap was returned to her by an irate woman in strict Muslim dress who had been eating at one of the restaurants. So our pleasant dinners were tempered by the stress of minding someone else's child at a distance. When we went to look at the child close up, we noticed he had a huge bruise on his forehead - but nothing worse than our son had had at that age. But we wondered if his mother was simple. There were also two dogs who lay down quite happily in the square and didn't seem to get run over either.

On two of the most punishingly hot days we gave up and went to the Ibis Hotel by the railway station, where, if you pay 90dh you can use the swimming pool and lie on lounge chairs. The pool water was delicious and there were lots of people swimming. All shapes of young women in bikinis sunned themselves but also a few women sat fully dressed with headscarves while their husbands and children frolicked in the pool.

During this hot time I read most of the books I had brought from America: *The Sea* by John Banville where the setting was Ireland and cool. I read *The Magician's Assistant* Ann Patchett and *Tales from the Arabian Nights* - which reminded me of Saturday morning cartoons with adventures galore and treasures and mysterious holes in the ground. Then *Esmond* by Thackery in a thin-papered leather bound edition. Then *The Magnificent Ambersons*. Each book taking me momentarily into another world away from the heat.

The day for the closing finally arrived and we went up to the notaire's office and sat looking at photos of him with the king at the sports club while we waited for Danny, the French owner of the little house to arrive. The translator, required by law, turned up and we smiled and nodded.

We had dressed up for the big occasion to look as respectable as possible whereas Danny, when he did get there, was wearing stylishly ragged designer jeans. The notaire's secretary wore white gloves and handed out multiple papers. The translator translated for our benefit, then more documents and money and papers exchanged hands. We paid the notaire. We paid the translator. We had to accept that everything was in order even if the actual title to the property as still in limbo. We shook hands with everyone except the secretary and the deal was done.

"So we own a house!" Robert and I grinned at one another.

Then Danny said we had to go to RADEEMA, the gas, water and light utility office, to get our names put on the bills. This proved impossible that day so we made a plan to meet at the next morning at Cafe France. We were pleasantly surprised that he was there.

Danny was waiting for Ismail the spidery young man who was his *guardien*. It must have been Ismail's thin arm I had spied the evening when we were snooping before we got in to the house.

All four of us set out for the RADEEMA offices in the medina where several dozen people were already waiting. Finally the multiple and multi-colored papers were signed after Ismail had had to go off to make copies of Robert's birth certificate, his passport and our marriage certificate in triplicate. Then an appointment was made to file all the papers at the main RADEEMA office in Gueliz. When I asked Danny why it couldn't be done all at once and he merely shrugged and said, "*E Maroc!*"

Back at derb Djedid we discovered that we had inherited Ismail who is now to be our *guardien* and general helper. He is twenty two, lives round the corner with his parents and brother, is utterly charming and likes motorbikes, computers, and beer and cigarettes when he can get them.

Because we had told Danny that we didn't want the contents of the house, he had taken us at our word and the house was entirely empty - even the giant refrigerator had vanished as well as most of the light bulbs.

There was a giant dead cockroach in the hall and two charming lizards in the salon - other than that nothing at all except the smell of drains. We sat on the ledge of the fountain in the courtyard and looked around us and pondered where on earth to begin. For one thing the colors were awful. The courtyard and the huge wall that stretched up to the terrace was yellow, as was the salon - but that was a different yellow. The downstairs bedroom, which later became my study, was Band Aid pink. The place was alarmingly dirty.

At the hardware store in the souks Robert bought a screwdriver and I bought two brooms.

A smartly dressed young Moroccan woman came up to me looking surprised. "Why are you buying those?" she asked, indicating the brooms. "Don't they have them in your city?"

I tried to explain that we weren't tourists but intended living there. We bought soap too and other cleaning supplies and set to work but were quickly utterly overwhelmed.

At Sherazade we explained our plight. We needed someone to help us clean up. Possibly more than one person. Ghislan, the pretty, round-faced chambermaid promised to meet us at four in the afternoon when she got off work. This was a blessing indeed.

As we waited for Ghislan at Cafe France, the usual people selling things went by and Robert was struck by a man with a bicycle with palm trees on the back of it. He immediately got up and bought one for 70 dirhams - the man had wanted 100. So we processed to the house and the palm tree seller carried the tree up to the roof. When he left we tried to remove enough of the dried up mud in one of the big pots Danny had left - probably because they were too awkward and heavy to move. It was exactly like trying to dig through concrete. We found a trowel which Robert used like a chisel - bashing it with an old tile which immediately broke. It was so hot we put wet wash clothes on our heads. When we tried watering the dirt, it became a viscous mud; in the end it took about an hour to plant the palm tree which had four healthy fronds and a fifth just coming in. It looked wonderful and cast cool shadows.

Then Ghislan, quite transformed in tight T-shirt and jeans and wearing shoes with heels, met us. Her French was almost as bad as mine. Her first language was Berber. But somehow we managed to communicate by smile and gesture. At the little house, she transformed herself once again into a maid, stashing her good clothes under the sink.

Ghislan and I then went the store on derb Dabachi which sold everything - plastic flowers, plastic trays, school bags, alarm clocks that looked like mosques. I told Ghislan to buy whatever we might need. This included *Flotta*, a green dishwashing detergent, numerous floor cloths, a plastic bucket and and a mysterious *produit* for cleaning the metal washbasins. I also bought a two burner gas stove made in Turkey. Ismail was summoned to bring a bombola of gas and hook it up to the stove. The bombolas come from a little shop in the alley which refills them and are wheeled to the house on the back of a bicycle shared by everyone in the derb. I bought milk and tea bags and sugar from the *hanut* -the little shop on the corner.

Ghislan, singing all the time, set about cleaning the house top to toe. She started on the roof, swept there, then watered the palm tree and the sad olive tree and worked her way downwards. When she got to the courtyard she ended up barefoot sloshing great pails of water about. Then she put wet cloths over the drains in the floor and the smell of medieval drains miraculously vanished.

Then the front door bell, which sounded like birds tweeting, rang and the two bed frames and two mattresses which we had ordered were delivered by a man with a hand cart. We tipped the man and he vanished. But how on earth were we to get the bed frames to the second floor when the stairs were so very narrow? Were we going to have to sleep on the ground floor?

In the end Ghislan, who is no more than five foot two, hauled the mattresses and frames up over the railing from the courtyard with Robert pushing from underneath. It was then that I realized that Ghislan could do anything.

I made made tea for the first time and the bombola didn't explode. Ghislan stowed her maid's costume and flat plastic work shoes back under the sink and went home. The house was clean and the drains didn't smell. *Alhamdulillah.*

Ghislan's efficient cleaning must have stirred up the carpenter ant population that swarmed on the bedroom floor landing. Robert bought Raid from the everything store on Dabachi where the teenaged twin girls who work there giggled at him. The Raid smelled toxic - was toxic - but better that the beams weren't chewed to pieces - if they weren't already.

We retreated to the roof to escape the fumes and we noticed some workmen on the roof of a house across the derb. They seemed to be painters. We smiled and nodded and their foreman asked if we needed some painting done too. Yes, obviously we did - lots of it. What joy it would be to be rid of the omnipresent yellow. We invited Sayeed over to our place and he wandered about computing all that needed to be done. Dusk fell and Sayeed handed us his estimate on the back of an envelope. Robert was aghast. He had misread the 'dh' at the end of the number as zeros in the dim light. It looked to be more than the cost of the house itself - but turned out to be about $150 dollars.

Wonderful! When could they start? What colors did we want? Well, mostly white and maybe Marrakshi pinkish for the terrace. We paid a little more for a 'special tint' to add to the paint for the terrace roof so we wouldn't be exactly the same color as everyone else.

So now we had a two burner camping gas stove, two bed frames and mattresses, two mugs we had bought from America and various cleaning supplies. Nothing to sit on except the edge of the little wall fountain in the courtyard, no tables to eat off, no fridge, no plates or utensils. It was very interesting to have nothing. It makes you think what the essentials are and how much stuff you have in your ordinary life that you don't really need - and how many things you can't do without.

We were still sleeping at Sherezade but spending the days at the the little house when not rushing round town trying to acquire the essentials - towels, tea spoons, saucepans and so on. The only sheets available in the souks were horrid and half nylon so we had to go out to Marjane, the French hypermarket outside town, to get cotton ones. We also bought a rather nasty plastic-handled flatware set - the kind most people use for picnics.

On derb Dabachi between Djemma Elfna and our little house, there is a woodshop - or rather a woodworkers' encampment down a little dirt and wood chip alley. Everything there was made by hand. The workman we chose was sitting on a huge pile of wood chips carving with an ax - his only tool. The first day we bought two little rush seated stools so we had something, however humble, to sit on. They cost five dollars each. The woodworker then showed us the four designs of dining chair he had. We ordered four and two days later went to collect them. Robert then drew the design for a table to put the alarming camping gas stove on and that was produced the next day. A couple of weeks later we augmented our chair supply with two arm chairs with rush seats, and the luxury of swivel backs - each about $15 and wonderfully comfortable.

Our dining table would be in the courtyard and open to the elements, so we designed one with tiles on top and a metal base. The tiles are inlaid in a simple pattern and are soft pink with a hint of green. This table top weighs at least a hundred pounds and took two weeks to make but is very beautiful. Robert designed and ordered two metal tables with glass tops for us to work on.

Something we came upon and didn't design at all is the absurd little round Berber table up on the terrace which looks as if it was painted with mustard. The old man who sold it to us at Bab Chemis the flea market laughed like mad when we agreed to pay $4 for it. At that price it seemed churlish to haggle.

Robert started to set up his studio in one of the upstairs bedrooms - the one with the Majorelle blue alcove. He also bought bird seed - *mekklah per tweer* - to feed the charming little birds on the roof.

The next morning Sayeed's crew arrived including a very young boy and a religious man with a beard who I didn't shake hands with. The painting commenced and the lemon yellow vanished from the courtyard and the pink from the downstairs rooms. The only problem was that the fumes from the paint made me feel sick - a sort of low level nausea that was debilitating and lasted for days. Robert went to the pharmacy and bought me some anti nausea medicine which seemed to work in the end. An enforced reducing diet on which I lost about seven pounds.

One afternoon when we got back from Cyber Park where we went to send emails, we noticed that the paint on the terrace wasn't the pink we had expected but the same old BandAid pink that it ever was. What happened to our special tint? Oh, Sayeed explained, we wouldn't like it. It wouldn't be good for our health. And he had painted all the terra-cotta pots on the terrace pink too.

The next afternoon we arrived at derb Djedid to discover Sayeed on the roof with an electrician explaining to him where all sorts of lights and outlets could be placed. He seemed to have appointed himself our general contractor. Robert said we didn't need half the stuff Sayeed wanted to do and pointed out what we *did* want: a light on the stairs, one in the hall and one over the front door and a new fuse box. Nothing more.

Then Robert went off to Cyber Park to do emails again and fight with Maroc Telecom whose promised telephone hadn't appeared. Robert left me to wait for Sayeed to return with the electrical bits and perhaps for the much longed-for and often promised telephone to appear. Ghislan was there and the five painters including the religious one, and Ismail too just to see what was going on. Life at 115 was becoming something of a local spectator sport. Little boys gathered in the alley and sometimes rang the door bell just to see what it sounded like.

Mohommed the electrician set to work and discovered that the light over the front door had faulty wires and it would require complicated diggings through two foot thick walls which was discouraging. Robert reappeared and said not to bother.

Mohommed then went out in to the derb with his metal ladder to tinker with the birds nest like coil of wires that dangled from the wall. A sudden flash of light - then no lights at all and Mohommed in a heap on the ground. Once recovered, he removed a bent piece of metal that had served as a fuse. Ismail was despatched to buy a porcelain proper one. Then Mohommed remounted the ladder, was promptly shocked again and the porcelain fuse smashed to bits on the ground. In the end the lights were restored by the replacement of the original bent piece of metal, which we had luckily saved.

By now there were at least twelve people in the house. I headed to the roof for some peace and quiet and an illicit cigarette. But there was the stout religious painter kneeling towards Mecca on his prayer rug. No cigarette.

Sayeed's wife, who I hadn't really needed to help with anything, was sitting on a stool in my study having swilled out the floor with bleach and used both of my American tea towels to mop up the mess. I felt very sorry for her, so said nothing about the ruined tea towels nor the sopping wet magazine. Sayeed asked if I wanted his wife to come back the next day and looked disappointed when I said that I didn't. She continued to sit on the stool with her eyes downcast.

When Sayeed, Mrs. Sayeed, the painters, the electrician, the assorted hangers on and Ismail and Ghislan and all the small boys had finally left, we sat on the roof and watched the swifts swooping through the dusk searching for mosquitos. Then the bats came out, night fell and the air was filled with the imam's call to prayer from the mosque. Everything peaceful at last.

We slept at Derb Djedid for the first time that night and awoke to the cries of the street vendor. *"Getta hut! getta hut!"* which we discovered was fresh fish - not a garden shed. When I went out into the derb to retrieve our nice new plastic dustbin, I discovered it had vanished. No *poubelle* for us from then on - just black plastic bags.

The little brown birds which Robert fed on the roof were delightful and inquisitive and started wandering round the bedroom and looking at me with their heads on one side. We decided to confine feeding them to the terrace.

Because the laundry near Sherezade tended to lose things, I started washing our clothes by hand in a blue plastic bucket and drying them on the roof where they dried in no time - including blue jeans which usually take ages and ages. Then one of my t-shirts vanished. It blew off the terrace into the traditional family's courtyard next door where I spied it lying on the ground. It was irretrievably gone since I didn't dare knock on their door, so I went out and bought pegs.

The two black metal work tables Robert had designed were delivered and were excellent. However, we would have to get someone to help boost Robert's work table over the railings as it won't fit up the stairs to his studio. We will have to wait for Ghislan for that. The telephone never appeared.

The doorbell tweeted and a painter, who said he had worked for Danny, appeared and offered to do anything. He had always worked on the house he said. We thanked him and took his phone number but said we really didn't need anything now. He left looking miserable.

The door bell tweeted again and a man, accompanied by his teenaged daughter, asked if I needed a *femme du menage*. I don't want a full time maid because the house is so small and the thought of someone being there all the time without much to do is depressing. The girl looked like a Florentine madonna and I wondered what it would be like to live in someone else's house far from home and unable to communicate much. So many people need work.

One of the delights of moving to Marrakesh was discovering how everyday things differ from at home. The first, and most obvious, was how plentiful and inexpensive fresh fruit and vegetables are – great heaping piles of little oranges, grapes, bananas, dates and olives in little hole-in-the-wall shops and on handcarts on every street. I bought fresh mandarins or oranges most mornings to squeeze to accompany either flat, round bread or baguettes just delivered from the bakery. You can get cereal including Frosted Flakes – my favorite – but since the milk is different, fruit, bread and apricot (*meshmash*)jelly are the best options.

In the covered market by the Mellah – old Jewish quarter – charming chickens, rabbits and pigeons hop in cages awaiting their doom. Some people take the birds home still alive suspended from their bicycle handles: at least they are certain the food is fresh. I don't think I could eat a creature whose beady eye had met mine.

The Mellah market also sells beautiful roses for only 20 dirhams for twenty (about $2.50). The vendors always throw in a few extra as a *'petit cadeaux'* – little gift. Often when I carry the flowers home I'm approached by a Moroccan who asks for one "*Pour moi?*" – and I'm happy to oblige.

For lunch we mostly have a picnic in our courtyard – bread and cheese and salad with bright red tomatoes, and olives of course, either spicy green ones or small black ones. In the afternoons carts appear with macaroons, napoleons and miniature croissants.

For dinner we often have chicken with whatever vegetable seems most abundant that day. I hadn't yet mastered the tagine – a melange of meat and vegetables arranged beautifully with the meat inside, slow cooked all day under a conical earthenware hat. Because you buy everything fresh, we were in Marrakesh for three months before we realized we needed a can opener. So, all in all, we had a very healthy diet with almost nothing packaged, frozen or canned. Everything is convenient and available within a five minute walk. The only things we have to go on a bus out of the old part of the city to get are bacon, hard cheese like Edam, and, of course, beer.

I had started cooking on the alarming two burner Turkish counter top stove. Most of my efforts were edible but dull so one evening we went to look for Catanzaro, the Italian restaurant in the Ville Nouvelle where we had eaten on visits to Marrakesh. We decided to take the bus from Djemma Elfna which was a mistake as it was going-home time with a great crush of people waiting to and rushing the doors all at once. Then we discovered we had lost Catanzaro and walked round in circles for half an hour getting more and more hungry and grumpy and had to cross a road with no traffic lights and wished to kill each other.

Ramadan

The first day of Ramadan fell on September 24th and Robert decided to celebrate it after encouragement from Ismail and Ghislan. During the night the incense seller went round scenting the streets and extracts from the Koran wafted across from the mosque. Robert got up at five after the early prayers in the dark and swigged two cups of coffee, two glasses of water and ate some some bread with *meshmash* jelly to fortify himself for the day ahead. Better to get up early, we were told, than have the devil kneel on your chest.

It was utterly quiet and peaceful in the early morning without a single moped. We went out to Djemma el Fna which was also quiet with no Moroccans eating or smoking, and only a very few tourists in the cafes.

We spent the morning in the spice market trying to buy big floor cushions to sit on. The first ones we liked a lot were orange and pink and Berberish - but absurdly expensive. The next one we quite liked and came to an agreement to pay three hundred dirhams for - but no stuffing came with the cushion. The seller insisted we could get it stuffed for four dirhams a kilo but when we went to the stuffing place they said it would be 20 dh for labor + about 40 dh for stuffing and the whole thing became too expensive and depressing, so we went and returned the cushion cover and, eventually, got our money back. So maybe it's better go to the artisans' exhibit place where the prices are fixed and they aren't allowed to harass you.

Then we walked home a new way past all sorts of fondouks being restored and got stuck in a human, donkey cart and moped traffic jam. The air was filled with moped fumes and light filtered slantwise through the slatted bamboo shades above us.

I had three small bananas for lunch but Robert had nothing - not even a drink of water - which I though both noble and stupid of him. He was determined to get the full Ramadan experience. The point of Ramadan, we were told, is that you understand what the poor man feels every day. Privately I thought that a poor man could probably get a drink of water somewhere but kept my quibbles to myself.

By four in the afternoon, I was planning dinner, and by five we were praying for sunset. At five fifteen I started chopping up vegetables and frying them so they would be ready to pop in the omelet. We eventually ate just as dark fell - just after seven - and the call to prayer came and the streets became quiet again because everyone had rushed home to eat. It was a delicious dinner. Robert had his croissant from this morning and some nuts and Coca Cola as well, and then we went out for ice-cream and then Robert ate an apple and we both had tea. And that was the first day of Ramadan.

The second day of Ramadan found Robert still determined to fast, and the morning again very quiet. A man arrived to remove the rickety old wooden door to the terrace and replace it with a steel security one - which entailed knocking whole sections of concrete and mud brick out and making the steps to the terrace impassable and filled with concrete dust. Apparently it would take a tank to get through the new door which has metal spikes which go six inches into the concrete on either side. Robberies most often occur when thieves clamber from roof top to roof top and sneak in from there.

Ghislan arrived to clean in the afternoon and swilled and swabbed with a will and made both the metal wash basins sparkling bright with her magic *produit* - which turns out to be vinegar. She refused even a sip of water even though the day was astoundingly hot.

Maroc telecom did not arrive and I couldn't get M. Mounir from the Cyber Park office on the phone - his number gave only either a busy signal or merely rang and he wasn't there. I walked over to see him in the afternoon but the office was closed so on the way back I bought two little yellow and orange daisy shaped flowers whose petals shut up in the night to plant in pots on the terrace.

The 4th day of Ramadan was not a good day, though I did manage to get some writing done in the morning.

Later, I walked the back way via Douar Groua into town and stopped and had a tour of Riad Noga - which we can see from our roof. It was a wonder - a huge riad with two courtyards beautifully decorated and there was a swimming pool in one with no visible edge, tiled in some mid-range color so it looked just like a courtyard pool - not a turquoise piscine at all. There were plants everywhere, billowing bougainvillea in pots and roses in vases and it was quite blissfully beautiful; the sort of place which makes you think Morocco is heaven - unlike rue Dabachi which at busy times resembles hell. M. Mounir, from Maroc telecom called three times asking for address confirmation - and then again at about three saying they were coming *"maintenant"* - but no one showed up so I was in a fury.

Robert started feeling really lethargic and pathetic at pretty much the same time as he has felt each day of his self-imposed fast. My cell phone - one I bought in Djemma Elfnaa - which does seem to work now - has come up with the message 'invalid battery' - a new one on me - so at about 4:30, realizing that *'maintenant'* wasn't about to happen, I walked to Djemma el Fnaa to ask the Medital people what was up - but Medital was closed. The day was very hot. While walking home, I passed the side of the souk where an argument broke out and a young man was threatening another with an upraised stool - really going for him as if he was about to bash his head in. This attracted an enormous crowd, but I left as I didn't think I could contribute anything positive to this. Tempers fray easily when you are very hot and very hungry.

So I hung around at home feeling fed up. Robert felt lousy but we were looking forward to going to Bodega for beer on tap and English Night. We had been looking forward to this for a week ever since we read about it in the "Best of Marrakech". So just after six we got cleaned up a bit and about half past six we set out.

We ran into Ismail in the derb and I told him our woes with Maroc Telecom and he said all three of us should go up tomorrow and yell at them and force someone to come back to the house with us. Then we walked on to the little Dabachi square where all the cats usually are and saw more men arguing. Three young men were restraining another and then I noticed that the one being somewhat restrained was holding a six-inch knife. Robert was quite oblivious to this but I yelled at him to turn back. I'm sure the quarrel had absolutely nothing to do with us - but what if the knife-wielding man broke lose and hated foreigners?

As we returned down derb Djedid we met Ismail again and he and another neighbor, who had heard about our Maroc Telecom woes, offered to go with us to a different office tomorrow and I imagined a huge posse of us threatening them. I did not think this would prove to be very useful.

By the time we had got to rue riad Zitoune dusk had fallen and it was as if the world had ended - the streets had completely emptied and even Djemma el Fna was almost deserted. At the bus stop there were a whole line of empty buses with the lights out and no passengers or drivers. Boulevard Mohammed V had about two cars on it instead of the usual thousands. It was almost spooky. We got a taxi to Charley's Cabana which had all the lights on but said *'Ferme'* so we decided to walk to Catanzaro where it was the same -

the manager was on the phone behind the desk but there were no waiters or customers. There were only two or three people walking about and, since Robert hadn't broken his fast yet, we were getting quite desperate for sustenance. Cafe Solaris had had a few foreign customers but they weren't being served since the waiters were watching the Haj on TV.

Eventually we found an open cafe and Robert ordered a mineral water and me an orange juice - the waiter brought my orange but said they had no water. So Robert got an orange juice too, and then we went to Catanzaro and ate lots and then discovered "Bodega" was utterly and permanently closed and so we abandoned any idea of being entertained during Ramadan.

Robert, finally, decided he had had enough of the Ramadan experience and decided to eat normally. This started with him buying a beautiful apple slice at a swanky bakery in Gueliz. As we carried it home down derb Djedid, the patisserie box attracted a crowd of small children yelling 'cookie' and touching the box and my handbag, and we had to fight them off at the door - actually an old lady came out and yelled at them. I would like to give the children something for Ramadan - but would giving one child something tiny escalate into having to give something to all the children in the neighborhood? Sadly, I think it would.

The next day the phone did not come either.

Alhamdulillah! The next day Aziz and a friend arrived to install the telephone. However he did not have our name on his list - instead it said Emilie Butt. We have no idea who Emilie Butt is, but told him to go ahead anyway. Aziz was carrying three new telephones but said he had no work order for us to have one - so I went off to see M. Mounir at Maroc Telecom at Cyber Park and he reluctantly gave me a silver telephone off the display. M. Mounir said that Aziz should have the DSL but he didn't and sent me to Maroc Telecom Centrale in Gueliz where I was to ask for Le Directeur, who eventually, after several phone calls, gave me a box with a DSL in it. The only thing is, neither the telephone nor the DSL work. Apparently, the telephone will work tomorrow - *Inshallah*!

The charming bird family were getting out of control. They started building a nest inside my study on the ground floor, so we now have to keep that door shut. In future they will only be fed on the roof - if at all.

I bought a pepper grinder because chopping pepper corns by hand is impossible. I was very excited since I had been looking for one for two weeks. I had to buy a salt shaker at the same time - the set cost 100dh - about $12.50. Unfortunately, when I got the grinder home I discovered there was no way to get the pepper corns into it.

We thought we would have a nice curry for dinner and went to the local spices man who sold us a small amount of 'Moroccan curry powder'. Robert spent a long time chopping vegetables and we fried up the ground beef and added the curry. The result was an inedible paste rather similar to the cement used for the new security door. Luckily I had sliced some cucumber in vinegar so we ate that then went out and had three scoops of ice-cream at Le Premices to take away the taste. We met Teresa and Justin, a young Canadian couple who were traveling round the world and who had just visited Damascus which sounded wonderful.

That evening when we went up to the roof we discovered a very friendly and pretty young cat had come to visit. She is a large kitten with orange, tabby and white markings and a long nose and eyes slanted up more than an American cat. She looks rather Egyptian.

The next day we walked into town, Robert tried out his new bank card and his *Code Confidential*, and, to our utter amazement, it worked. Then we went to see the man who sold me the pepper grinder and gave it to him to see if he could find a way to put the peppercorns in. He couldn't, so I left it with him. When we returned an hour later, he was still fiddling with it. So, I suppose he's still trying to make it work.

In the plant section of Djemma el Fna I bought a plumbago, a jacaranda, and some sort of vine with pretty fragrant pink flowers, three large pots and two sacks of dirt. These were loaded onto a hand cart and trundled through the square. I paid the porter extra to carry everything up to the roof and he was very pleased.

I tried out the silver telephone and got a dial tone. I managed to call the landline from my cell phone but can't make any calls out. I then got through to some sort of service place. About an hour later six smartly dressed young people with badges arrived from Maroc Telecom asking if I had a problem. They filled the house and said Aziz, who had installed the telephone, wasn't a technician - but *they* knew how to fix it. "Moose", a very slight young, man took the DSL connection apart with a kitchen knife and then put it together again. While the house was filled with the Maroc Telecom technicians, there was a knock at the door and I opened it to two tall young men in ankle length robes. One of their robes was bright scarlet and he carried a six foot metal horn which he blew very loudly and then asked for money. I went and asked the Maroc Telecom technicians whether I should give money to the medieval musicians and they said yes so I gave them 5dh.

The technicians said M. Mounir should have given us a contract and a password but since it was the weekend we wouldn't be able to have the Internet until Monday when they would return and set it up. However, we were now able to receive calls and Bobby called from New York. It was lovely to hear his voice.

      We potted all the plants then had a safe cheese and vegetable omelet for supper. When we went up to the roof to drink our tea, Mimi, the little cat, reappeared - all cats seem to be called Mimi here. She ate a little of Robert's almond croissant and then vanished down the stairs into the house. We sat by the light of the metal lantern and looked at the very bright stars - none of which we could identify. When I eventually found Mimi in the hall and picked her up to carry her back to the terrace, she purred cheerfully. The birds seem to to have vanished - perhaps they are mad at us - or Mimi.

      We went out early to buy bread and there were only a few stale loaves from yesterday. The young man said fresh bread was coming soon but the bakers were still asleep - I think Ramadan tires people out - all that feasting in the evenings and late into the night.

      We made a trip to Marjane and were amongst the first people there. We stocked up on more sheets and towels and hard cheese and beer - we should have had ID for the liquor, but since it was pretty obvious to the young man that we weren't Moroccan we were grudgingly allowed to have it after he wrote all our details down in his ledger.

      In the afternoon a suit-clad salesman came to the door and wanted to give me a free sample of shampoo, but I told him I didn't want it because, had I taken it, he might call every week and I'd end up with bottles and bottles of the stuff just because I had felt sorry for him.

      It was very warm when we went to the internet place and when walking home met Justin and Teresa, the Canadians, and invited them to tea here. We sat on the roof and had tea and cake and chatted until it was dark and there were a lot of stars out. It was fun having English speaking people to talk to and to show the house to. These were our first non-Moroccan visitors.

We do not have the Internet yet but we do have a dining table. It was designed by Robert and made by the man who made our desk bases. It is rectangular and the top is done in natural colored tiles - all pretty much the same but with subtle variations. The top probably weighs at least 150 lb. It is a great treat to sit in the courtyard eating off a real table rather than on our knees.

Yesterday was a horrible day when everything went wrong and I felt like packing it all in and saying I couldn't stand it any more. First, I went to the laundry at nine and they weren't open yet. Then, I had endless fights with Maroc Telecom about the Internet and people kept saying they were coming over to fix it and no one turned up. I really don't mind waiting in for people if they eventually arrive. I hate waiting for people who have absolutely no intention of it. All the time, there was a cat howling incessantly from the adjacent roof top.

Next, I went past the woodcarver's shop to tell him to leave the little carved bedside table we had chosen unvarnished and he said he would leave it natural - but that it really wasn't his shop but his brother's - he produced a laminated card to prove it - and said that his brother wanted him to charge six hundred dirhams for it. Robert, already infuriated by the cat, went round and told the wood carver's brother that we had agreed on five hundred, but re-appeared reasonably cheerfully having waited for the real woodcarver to come back from the mosque. They had again agreed upon five hundred and then hugged and so forth.

In the evening we went to look for a Cyber cafe to use the internet and most of them were shut. A nice Australian girl pointed us in the direction of one and I noticed she was quite covered in bug bites - far worse than mine - and I asked her what hers were and she said bedbugs. She said her hotel had changed her room. I'm not certain merely changing rooms would solve the problem. I decided my bites are mosquitos and resolved to stop itching them. We looked at the posters outside the cinema and they were for *The Brothers Grimm* with Matt Damon - in French.

The next day was much better. Lo and behold! Maroc Telecom called me - rather than the other way round - and a perfectly competent person called Abdellah arrived and took everything apart and said that the problem was noise on the phone line and he would come back on Monday morning to fix it. I haven't the least idea why I believed him, but I did.

Then a man with a bicycle rang the doorbell and sold me one of the huge palm trees he was carrying on the back of it. So now we have two palm trees. One is never quite sure who will be there when the doorbell rings.

Having quite exhausted the reading matter I had brought from America (except *Emerson's Essays*) and the meager supply of lurid, much thumbed thrillers on Sherazade's shelf, I realized that getting hold of books was going to be a problem. Reading and talking about books is one of my chief delights, so once I sort of had a home phone with a semi-working number I decided to put a postcard in the window of the stationery store in Gueliz saying "English woman living in the medina seeks to start book group". I didn't hold out much hope for this but, to my delight, one afternoon as I was working in my study the phone rang for the first time.

"This is Judy Flahety. I saw your notice at the stationers. We already have a book group. I'll meet you at cafe Solaris on Tuesday." This was excellent news. Judy, a teacher at the American School, was small, red-haired, brightly dressed and very welcoming. Originally from Chicago, Judy has a house in Ireland but rents here. She lives with her husband Richard who is retired, left- wing and bookish.

After chatting at Solaris for a little while and inviting me to join the book group, Judy took me to Cafe du Livre a little hidden-away upstairs bookshop/cafe run by Sandra the wife of the headmaster of the American School. Here there was a most peculiar hodgepodge of used books - the sort of books people take on holiday and don't want to bother to take home, books on Middle Eastern history and photography and design and also the sort of dull books one wonders if anyone read ever. Judy told me she would keep in touch and let me know when anything interesting was going on in the evenings.

I spent the early evening gardening on the roof where it was over 90F but satisfying somehow. The second palm tree was planted and the papyrus re-potted but we need more dirt. Unfortunately you cannot buy potting soil but only huge sackfuls of dusty clay which are incredibly heavy and contain lots of rocks and sticks and other extraneous matter of dubious origin. You have to hire a man with a handcart to haul them round.

To celebrate Ramadan derb Dabachi is full of people selling day old chicks - dyed pink, blue or yellow - to little children who are thrilled with them. They do look and sound very charming as they hop round in their cardboard boxes. But what happens tomorrow when most of them are dead? I suppose the cats will have a feast day. I really don't want to think about it.

When we were fixing up the house, a neighbor often came to watch usually carrying his lovely runny-nosed toddler daughter and accompanied by his polite son of about nine of ten who liked to do little errands for us. Mustafa was a tall handsome man of about forty usually wearing a red sweater and blue jeans. Obviously no long conversations were possible, but we chatted in limited French. Unlike in New York, one never asks what anyone does but exchange pleasantries about weather and family and Maroc Telecom.

    One night we were crossing the square heading home in the dark, Robert was clamped on the shoulder by a vast and imposing fellow dressed in flowing blue Tuareg robes and wearing a turban. "*Sahhibi*!" he cried and Robert jumped assuming it was someone trying to sell him something he didn't want.

    Then we discovered it was our neighbor Mustafa in his full work costume, and he invited us to visit his shop - the three square feet of carpet where he sells potions and ostrich eggs and strange minerals in glass bottles. By the flickering lamplight, he made up a potion one for Robert's leg - the one mangled from a long ago accident. He gave it to us for nothing and Robert massaged the unguent on to his scarred leg.

    And that was the end of our first month in the little house.

October

I decided to go to church, not because I'm religious, but more to see what it would be like. The Roman Catholic church in Gueliz was built in 1926 opposite a mosque whose design is not dissimilar. It had said in one of the guidebooks that there was a Protestant service at 10:30 in a hall opposite - but there wasn't - so I joined the congregation in the Roman Catholic one - mostly French families with children and older French people who were sitting on ordinary sort of wood pews. The altar was decorated with white roses and yellow and pink stained glass threw pretty lights into the nave. The service was conducted in French, by three African priests and two European ones and I could sort of understand what was going on. The choir, sitting above the organ loft consisted of young African women who sang enthusiastically and wonderfully loud and the hymns were extremely cheery. At the end of the service I bought two little embroidered handkerchiefs which were being sold for charity in the lobby.

As far as I could discover, the only other English speakers were a middle-aged couple from St. Louis - she was a Methodist minister and he retired. They were pleasant and chatty, but as a social event it was rather a bust.

October 2, 2006

We had a lot of business things to accomplish, so took the bus up to Gueliz at about 9 am. We had breakfast at the Snowball Cafe then went to the bank where there was a huge crowd of people. We realized that since it was the first business day of the month people were waiting in line for their pensions - or anyway some sort of payment. Miss Snippy, the bank teller, grudgingly showed Robert how to write a Moroccan check - money at the top where we would put the date and you have to write the city in too. But she wouldn't give us any money and casually waved us in the general direction of the almost line of about thirty people. She looked rather pleased we would have to wait a long time. So we waited until someone said that a somewhat shorter line was for people with checks to cash rather than some other sort of payment. I looked daggers at a man who pushed to the counter ahead of us. But we did eventually get our money.

When we went to look at the art materials shop but they did not have a very good selection - for example the oil paints had no yellows at all. Then we went to a travel agent to try to get cheap tickets to Milan in November - since we have to leave the country every ninety days for passport reasons. The first travel agent only found a hideously expensive fare and the second one was a young woman who took a long personal telephone call and didn't seem very interested, so we went to Royal Air Maroc which was much more efficient and the young woman spoke English. We are now going to Milan and Florence at the end of October for a week on Atlas Blue.

Our next stop was the office of M. le Directeur of Maroc Telecom to explain our various woes. He handed us off to an English speaking colleague who led us to a Kafka-esque adjacent building where we went up to the third floor and he explained that as non-residents we would have to pay a year's worth of Internet fees up front. This is about two hundred dollars so we said that was OK - but we would have to pay another visit to my friend M. Mounir in Cyber Park - who perhaps could have told us all this two weeks ago. There was the usual huge crowd of people waiting outside the building and we felt a little guilty that as foreigners we seemed to get better treatment - but, of course, we still didn't have the internet.

Next we walked to the notaire's office and handed in the copy of our marriage certificate and our letters - one in English, one in French, saying that 115 derb Djedid was our second home and not our principal residence. This is something to do with taxes.

As a reward for all this rushing about, we went to lunch at the Grand Cafe de la Poste and sat on the side terrace and were misted with a fine spray of water which cooled the air. I don't think I've ever been in 90F heat in October before. Having eaten lunch in a very swanky place, we went home on the bus and later ever-cheery Ghislan appeared and washed the floors - so altogether a day where much was accomplished.

The internet still doesn't work - password problems - but Ismail came over and showed me how to re-charge the phone using the code on a little plastic card I bought on derb Dabachi so we could now call out! I chatted to Claud in London. Two internet geeks showed up in the afternoon and said I would have to take my computer to Cyber Park to see the dreaded M. Mounir tomorrow. This is all getting too horribly dreary - both to live through and to read about. I have no confidence whatsoever in this latest plan, and think someone should come here. I then telephoned Bobby in New York and Robert chatted for twelve minutes and our first hundred dihram card ran out.

Still very hot and still Ramadan.

Ismael's mother is sending over some harira soup this evening which is very kind of her. The family lives just round the corner which is pretty convenient. When the guns had gone off signaling the time for the *fitur*, Ismael came back with the promised soup and dates and honey pastries and some curious powdery stuff - very sweet and nut flavored - which he said you ate with the *the* Lipton. Everything was beautifully presented on a tray with a saucepan of hot soup, two large wooden soup spoons, and two little bowls. Harira is a traditional Ramadan treat - a vegetable soup with a lamb broth base with beans and every veggie you can think of - a meal in itself. His mother, he said, was a very good cook would make us tagines and roast chicken if we ever wanted - all we had to do was pay for the ingredients. Robert loved the dates and tried the powdery nut stuff which he put in his tea but later gave up on - perhaps you are meant merely take a pinch of it on the side.

October 13, 2006

The other day we were just settling to have a nap after lunch when there came a loud knocking on the front door. We couldn't think who it was. When Robert opened the door, he discovered a small excited man who explained - sort of - that Mohammed had gone to the hospital and he was collecting for him. Which Mohammed? Who? Robert said the small excited man had obviously rung every bell on the street since everyone was looking out.

This was the first time since an old woman's funeral thee weeks ago that we had been asked for local charity, so we thought we would like to give something - even though we still didn't have the least idea who Mohammed was.

Robert called up to me, indicated to the man to wait in the hall, and went into the studio to look for money. Meanwhile, barely dressed, I got up to see what was going on, to discover the small man, upstairs, looking in through the bathroom window at me. He had followed Robert upstairs and kissed me on the cheek on the landing.

We managed to get him downstairs, gave him some money - for which he seemed very grateful - and he then kissed us both on both cheeks and left like a whirlwind. We never saw him again.

That evening we went to the opening of an exhibition of lithographs at the French Institute in Gueliz which we had been told about by Judy Flaherty. The event was posted as opening at eight but the whole place looked utterly deserted when we arrived about 7:45. We are always too early for everything. So we sat on a bench in the courtyard and looked at a gang of large kittens fighting with one another. Then one older and artsy looking couple turned up and we went in and looked round the prints which were mostly big name 20th century European - Dali, Leonor Fini, Chagall and so on and some Moroccan. As usual we had 'done' the show in about fifteen minutes. We explored the modern building again and then sat in the courtyard again to see if Judy would turn up. By eight thirty, few other people were there so we decided to leave. As we were walking down the street we met Judy, wearing a bright red dress, so we went back and suddenly quite a lot of people arrived and waiters handed round hot mint tea in little glasses and also cocktail snacks. Judy, who seems to know everyone, introduced us to David Hales an Englishman who lives in the Medina. So it was worth going to in the end. We were, finally, learning that in Morocco being prompt is quite useless.

We walked back to Boulevard Mohammed V past lots of cafes with men sitting drinking coffee and chatting. I assumed all their wives were at home.

We decided to take Ismail up on his offer to have his mother cook a tagine for us. He arrived about six thirty to set the table and folded the napkins into fans - he once worked in a restaurant. He brought Moroccan salad -cooked tomato and pepper and cilantro and spices - and all the fixing for Moroccan tea: black tea which looks like little black granules, huge lumps of sugar called lingots and fresh mint to seep in the black tea.

Ismail came back at seven carrying the big, round tagine dish with conical lid on a straw tray. He revealed its contents with a flourish; on the top were all the vegetables: tomatoes and potatoes and zucchini arranged very beautifully, underneath it was the chicken breast, steeped all day in herbs and spices. He had also bought a round, flat loaf of homemade bread. It was the best tagine I've ever had and enough for two days at least. He then went home to have his dinner and then reappeared about eight to make sure we had enjoyed the tagine and make mint tea.

When he put seven large lingots of sugar into the pot, I suggested that Mr. Robert didn't like it quite so sweet.

"*E diabet?*" Ismail asked looking worried.

No, not *diabet* - yet.

When we go up to the roof about seven thirty in the morning, everything is utterly quiet. As we water the plants, regarding each one very carefully, there are birds tweeting, the sky is always getting blue - and sometimes the moon is still there. If you look across all the roof tops, you can see which houses have Europeans in - they are the ones with the roof gardens and palm trees and bougenvillia. Most Moroccans don't use their roofs as gardens but hang the laundry there and store broken bicycles, dead refrigerators and other assorted junk. Most houses have ugly satellite dishes.

The skyline is mostly of buildings, some with crenellated walls. You can see mosque towers including the Kotubia and a few tall palm trees. The Atlas mountains are only visible sometimes. I think they are more often seen when they have snow on in the winter.

Walking down rue Dabachi, between Djemma el Fna and derb Djedid, at nine in the evening is like going to the circus or

Fellini's film *Amarcord*. All the shops are still open and it is thronged with hundreds of people of all ages, bicycles, mopeds, donkey carts and caleches. Little boys play soccer, teenage ones with gelled hair lounge about looking cool, beggars are abject, girls giggle with their friends. The dim young woman in *Kotubia Pressing* fails to find anyone's laundry.

    As well as the shops, street vendors sell bright, brittle plastic toys, very cheap underwear, Dolce & Gabbana handbags, CD's, pomegranates, grapes, tagine dishes, wonderful pastries and pretty much everything else you can imagine. Some people lay all they possess out on the ground - worn jeans, old shoes, used utensils - in the hopes that perhaps someone might want them. There is a table with goats' heads and trotters. The cheeping, doomed dyed chicks still sound very cheerful and look lovely hopping about all together in their cardboard boxes.

    The shops on rue Dabachi are mostly very small - scarcely larger than big cupboards - but manage to contain all sorts of important items like shampoo, Vache Qui Rit cheese, and milk which comes in squishy white plastic bags which you have to cut the corner off with scissors incredibly carefully so you don't spill it everywhere. There is one slightly bigger shop presided over by a most charming older man in a yellow smock who teaches Robert lots of words in Arabic. Between each item of your order he says *bismallah* and then his bespectacled and brown smocked assistant climbs up a ladder to retrieve if is it is on a high shelf. When you buy eggs in the souks you are given them in flimsy plastic bags bags too and you have to hope you don't bash into anything taking them home.

    Yesterday we got a bill for $15 from Maroc Telecom for the instillation of the telephone. It was addressed to Emilie Butt.

We went out early to get orange juice and a croissant near the cinema - hiding from anyone who might know us and realize we were cheating on Ramadan. It was a nice cool morning and I almost enjoyed the arrival of the sun. The usual parade of people passed by - including the plump, insistent beggar woman who approached us twice. Lots of people were looking at the piles of newspapers but not buying them. A man on a bicycle sold xeroxed copies of the crossword and puzzle page. It was not our usual waiter and we had to wait ages to pay, and, when he finally gave us change, it was 50 dh short. I think the waiter expected us not to notice, and eventually shuffled through his pocket and reluctantly gave us a few more coins. Still short, so we won't go there any more.

The covered market by the Mellah is full of chickens and roosters in cages and smells awful but is utterly fascinating. Some of the imprisoned birds are very beautiful. All the separate stalls have hand-painted notices saying white chickens, eggs, rabbits and roosters with pictures of each. Light was slanting in through the roof in beams full of motes of dust.

There were all sizes of fish and men in rubber boots swabbed down the slimy floor. A man dropped a vast, glistening fish onto the puddled floor, picked it up by a fin and put it back on the counter.

I bought bananas, lemons and apples and then went back to buy roses from Aziz who had given me a sample one the other day. They cost roughly ten cents each and smell beautiful and you fill the house with them. The only trouble was I hadn't got any vases and ended up putting them in jelly jars. As I carried a little arrangement of them up the stairs to the studio, I thought of the word 'nosegay' and realized that probably it came from medieval times - a little bunch of herbs and flowers would cheer your nose up. They give you mint to sniff when you visit the tannery. But that's another story.

Marrakesh is chock full of cats but there are very few dogs. Apparently the Prophet liked cats - so perhaps it's a little like cows in India. At first you think that the cats are all strays and then you realize that most of them are clean and sleek and have their own little territories and probably homes. The female cats are rather slim (when not pregnant) and have elegant pointed faces; the tom cats tend to be big, paler colored and with much wider faces and look pretty tough. Often there are almost white cats with dark tails and heads - possibly with some Siamese forebears.

The cats come in all different colors: marmalade, tabby, tuxedo, white, long haired and short haired. There are kittens all over the place - especially near butchers and fish sellers. One cat always follows *'getta hut'* man on the bicycle who sells fish door to door. She picks up the fish heads he drops for her. Some cats are very friendly but many other wary.

An enormously pregnant tortoise shell one lives by the shoe mender on the corner of rue Dabachi and derb Djdid. We have expected her to have kittens for the last three weeks -it must happen any day now.

Inside my white skirt the label said: Cold wash. No bleach. But the skirt was getting dingy so I washed it with a little bleach. It remained dingy so I soaked it in ONY from the corner *hanut* which I think is something like Oxyclean. There was little improvement. So I decided to dye it. I thought of making it a charming pink with beetroot and then wasn't sure it would work so we went to the dyers' souk to see what we could get there where they dye almost everything - mostly leather and fabric. They have vast vats of the stuff and the dyers' arms are all sorts of different colors. There are strips of fabric hanging from the roofs and billowing in the sunshine.

I wondered if there was a place you could drop things off to be dyed but couldn't find one, so went into a little shop where there was jar upon jar of powder dye - some made with cocheneil - the most expensive - and every other color you can imagine. The man in the shop said the traditional blue dye I liked was two dirhams a gram which sounded cheap - but then said I needed a hundred grams of the stuff which seemed quite mad. Twenty two dollars to dye one skirt which really, after all it had gone through, wasn't worth half that. Meanwhile the shopkeeper was busily spooning dye into a plastic bag.

Robert stood outside in his white shirt, which, for some reason, marks him out as someone to try to sell stuff to, and looked grumpy, and the dye seller asked if my husband was keeping Ramadan.

Of course I ended up with far too much dye anyway. Robert said I should take someone shopping with me in future since I was so hopeless at bargaining. I am hopeless at it, and pay too much for almost everything. But the skirt looks very pretty now - a soft blue like the plumbago and I managed to get out the coffee I spilled on it this morning.

This morning we got up very early to walk to the outside of the city to try to take photographs of the mountains without any antennas being in the way. We left the house before seven and walked to the *bab* (city gate) at the end of Dabachi. But we couldn't find a way to climb up on the city walls and it was rather overcast anyway, so we walked back through streets we were unfamiliar with which hadn't yet been paved with cobblestones like the smarter parts of town where houses and riads are being done up left and right. We saw three dogs out looking for food.

They had nice long legs, unlike the black and white dog who lies about in Djemma el Fna and has almost no legs at all. All the cats were waiting for the shop keepers to open up.

In the afternoon I decided pretend to be Emilie Butt and pay the bill for the phone installation. Not wanting to encounter the dreaded M. Mounir, I went to the Post Office in Djemma Elfna and was directed to station #8 which had about ten people waiting. The clerk behind the counter looked bewildered by his computer and was having a lengthy discussion with several of his co-workers. I noticed that in addition to taking the telephone money it was also the station for sending money orders abroad. After I'd waited about twenty minutes, a plump young man inserted himself in front of me in the sort-of queue at the counter. If I wasn't a foreigner I would have said something, but didn't. Judy Flaherty has a useful phrase, *"Ana luel. Ente tane!"* - I'm first. You're second. I'm much too timid to risk it.

I thought perhaps they would take the money at the Maroc Telecom booth in the square but they only sold mobile phone cards. I knew there was a Maroc Telecom office not too far away beyond Hotel Tazi. So I crossed a busy street and walked there to discover that, contrary to the posted signs, it was *mestdud* (closed) even through there were some people inside. A pleasant young Moroccan woman and I studied the posted times and rolled our eyes, and so I went back to the main post office and decided to enjoy waiting there. I studied all the people and the decor: pale green walls with the requisite framed portrait of the king, sample mailing boxes hanging looking a little tired. I thought the man in front of me in the queue was wearing a turban, but on closer inspection it turned out to be a bandage; his aged mother signed a document with a mark rather than a signature. One of the gray plastic seats clattered to the floor when a woman stood up.

When it was finally my turn, after almost everyone else had been helped, the clerk gave me a handwritten receipt because the machine wasn't working right. The ascetic thin faced man behind me in the line was wearing a brown suit and looked straight from the 1940's. Unlike me, he was not a bit impatient.

We have both recently read Peter Mayne's *A Year in Marrakesh* an account of his time spent there in the 1950's. What struck us most was how little things have changed in the way of interactions between people and the Moroccan's insistence on being helpful - even when one doesn't particularly want to be helped. Almost all Moroccans can be relied upon to have an opinion on whatever it is you think you want to do - where to keep your sugar, how many oranges you want to buy, what color to paint your room, the effect your light fixtures have on your health - and so on.

I'm beginning to understand the importance of greeting people you know on the street, the *salaam aleikum* - peace be upon you, *la bas*, which means "no harm" -or I hope everything is going well, to which you reply, *"becheer al'hamdollah or alhamdulilah* - roughly "I'm fine, thanks be to God'. Men usually shake hands with each other. Some men shake my hand but others merely nod and touch their hearts.

Inshallah - if God wills it - is a very useful term. As in -We will meet tomorrow at noon, *inshallah*. Well, if we do meet, God willed it, if we don't meet, God must have willed us not to meet - so that's all right too - it's quite out of our hands.

Peter Mayne spent a lot of time at Cafe France writing a now-lost novel and we long to go back there when Ramadan is over when we are not pretending to be keeping the daytime fast. Mayne's book is altogether most entertaining and beautifully written. His novel was never published but his diary remains a classic.

    Garrett and Jennifer, friends from New York, are staying in Marrakesh, so we took them to Dar Mimoun where we were sorry not to see the guinea fowl - perhaps it was eaten. We spent the afternoon at the Ben Youssef Medersa - a Koranic school with Carrara marble pillars, a reflecting pool and students' little cells decorated with elaborately carved cedar and plaster. Much more luxurious than the monks' cells in S. Marco in Florence. The ancient *guardien* followed us around making endless comments in his five word English vocabulary and wanting a tip. As far as we could gather the students spent five years at the medersa and the upperclassmen lived higher up in the building.

    Garret and Jennifer seemed entranced with Marrakech which made us happy - not that it's our responsibility at all. I'm sure it's not to everyone's taste and some things, like the beggars, are hard to take, but, all in all, in spite of the grittiness, there is something lovely about it.

    On derb Dabachi I saw the sad remnants of one of the once cheery dyed chicks. Vain to imagine they could survive all the attentions of the little children - not to mention the cats.

    A film seems to be going to be shot somewhere nearby. Rue Dabachi is full of lighting equipment and important people rushing around with laminated badges saying CREW. Ramadan is almost over.

    One day an official little note printed in Arabic is slipped through the letter box. Since we haven't the least idea what it means and can only decipher the date, we set it aside. A few days later while Robert is painting and I'm out, two men arrive at the door and ask whether Robert has any red paint. Of course he does and produces a jelly jar full of it. The men have come to take some sort of survey - something to do with the title of the house which is still in limbo. They take the red paint and make marks on the interior and exterior walls marking the bounds of our property. Our kitchen, it seems, goes under part of the religious people's house and all our utility meters are beyond the bounds of what we thought was ours. We cannot quite fathom why the surveyors didn't bring any red paint with them if it was needed - what if Robert wasn't a painter? Anyway, the survey was completed and we now have title to 115. And that was October.

November

Because of visa requirements we have to leave Morocco every ninety days. We decided to go to Italy for all sorts of reasons - to buy art materials, eat wonderful food, and, most of all, because we love it.

We left Marrakech very early in the morning and walked through the deserted streets where people sleep in doorways - kept warm by cats.

The plane followed the coast of southern France and it was like looking at Google Earth. Then we saw the snow capped Alps as we approached Milan.

Florence was wonderfully familiar. We ate at long remembered restaurants and drank quantities of red wine, which, without all the sulfites they put in it for export, slips down very easily.

After Marrakech, Florence seemed crisp, clean and prosperous. It was awash with tourists and now you have to pay to go into S. Croce and the front doors are kept closed. We didn't even attempt to go into the Uffizi for which you have to buy tickets in advance. Years ago it was free on Sundays and you could just wander in. Even the Boboli Gardens require a ticket now.

The weather was warm and lovely but definitely autumnal - I kept thinking of Milton's *'thick as autumn leaves which fill the brooks in Vallombrosa'*. Crunchy leaves underfoot.

In S. Marco we looked at the Fra Angelicos and compared the building with the Medersa in Marrakesh - both have austerely beautiful cells inviting contemplation. In the church of S. Marco, which is 19th century and pretty hideous, we had a long conversation with a white haired priest and told him Robert and I had met in Florence over thirty years ago.

He said, "Ah that was when Florence was Florence." Hearing we were from New York, he picked up the collar of his robe to reveal all sorts of American flag pins and told us that the Americans were very kind to him at the end of the war. We said of course many American people were wonderful - but the government was rather a different story. He was horrified when we said we lived in Marrakech among Muslims. We said that surely God made everyone - to which he was reluctantly forced to agree. He then discussed the French, who he wasn't fond of either. A garden center across the street had lots of cyclamen and other autumn flowers.

Robert watched the Ducatis win the motorcycle GP on a wide screen TV at the hotel bar. Odd to see CNN and BBC World bashing on about the same old stuff which doesn't seem to have too much to do with our lives any more - distant in time and space and rather sad. I am reading Alan Bennett's *Untold Stories* which spoke about the vanished England of the 50's and 60's. So altogether a nostalgic week.

In Milan, which was rather grim and forbidding with cold winds from the Alps, we found ourselves homesick for Marrakesh.

We arrived home to find all the plants on the roof flourishing and having grown in our absence and the house very neat and tidy and our beds decorated with rose petals. Ismail arrived about ten minutes after we did carrying a fresh bunch of roses which he arranged and put all over the house.

Rosie and Greg, old friends from England, arrived about six o'clock having driven over the Atlas and explored the south of Morocco. What pleasure to have very old friends to stay who seem to like our house too. Good to be able to share things we enjoy - including the one bottle of red wine we brought home.

Ismail from Sherazade telephoned and said the people there had missed us.

November 5, 2006

This afternoon in Djemma el Fna I saw the ideal stocking stuffer: a little plastic railway track with Osama bin Laden - in a white turban - in a little truck being followed by George Bush in a tank going endlessly round in circles. Needless to say this toy was made in China.

I discovered that the ancient husband of the nice woman in The-Laundry-that-does-not-Lose-Things comes from Reggio Calabria - so we had a little chat in Italian. He said Marrakech is not what it used to be.

Although I am very warm in just a t-shirt, the Marrakshis have busted out the winter jackets and sweaters. You can buy leopard skin patterned long johns to wear under your jellaba. I might get tempted.

November 12, 2006

After arriving too early for the art show at the French Institute a few weeks ago, we don't rush to openings any more. An eighty year old German painter, Geerdts, who has lived here for forty years, has a show at Dar Cherifa, where rose petals float in a small square sunken pool surrounded by candles in the middle of a vast Berber palace.

The paintings are whimsical. A great crush of people, with some Europeans wearing traditional Moroccan dress which seems a bit odd. The flowing robes threaten to catch fire in the candles.

At one point, Geerts, who walks with a cane, planted it firmly on Robert's foot, leant on it and started a long conversation with someone.

Tall white robed helpers with red hats handed round mint tea and Moroccan pastries. The German consul gave a slightly too long chat and many videos were made.

The next *vernissage* we attended - at Galerie Re in Gueliz - was quite an event. We were greeted by white-faced mimes on stilts, dressed as moths or butterflies or angels with huge white wings. They smiled and winked and drew a crowd of local onlookers who couldn't believe their eyes. The ex-pats were all there for the champagne and the stunning pastries. There were lots of hipsters, a model in high boots, and assorted other people all trying to impress one another and almost all talking French. The paintings were quite ignored in all the excitement. We were given a scented sachet with the gallery's card which later adorned our dingy downstairs bathroom. On the way home we checked out Tazi's bar.

Another social event was Tahir Shah's reading at Cafe du Livre, the English bookshop. It was *The Caliph's House*, Shah's splendid account of restoring a mysterious old house in Casablanca, that finally pushed us over the edge into buying in Morocco. Despite his exotic name, Tahir Shah came across as utterly English - he grew up in Tunbridge Wells after all. He began the reading by saying that almost everyone in the room probably had a similar story to tell which was probably true since Sandra's cafe was packed with a mostly English speaking crowd - most of whom were in the throes of doing up riads and dars. There was a long discussion about djinns and exorcisms. I told Tahir that if anything went horribly wrong with our house we would hold him personally responsible…

The only drawback to this entertaining evening was the fact that there were no copies of *The Caliph's House* to be bought or signed. The whole shipment was held up at customs in Casablanca.

November 18, 2006

My brother and his wife arrived on Wednesday evening. I went out to the airport to meet them and although it was past the time for them to arrive, their flight was not posted as *'arrive'*. I waited about a bit and then they walked through the exit - no one had bothered to write in the arrival on the board. I ordered the taxi to take us to Douar Groua - the Lycée end of derb Djedid so we could avoid derb Dabachi at its jostling evening finest. My brother, who tends to shun crowds, might have turned tail and gone straight back to England.

As I led Peter and Liz through the twisting lane, Liz asked how on earth I knew where I was going and I felt rather smug and local and familiar. Robert had put candles all over the hall - to make our house look like the mysterious east. We have given them our bedroom with its attached bathroom and are sleeping downstairs.

On Thursday it poured with rain and we sat in the salon watching the courtyard fill up with water. It reminded me of summers in Cornwall and smelled rather similar. Later I bought an umbrella from one of the umbrella salesman who had sprung up mushroom-like in the square.

In the evening we saw a man with a live chicken sitting on his head, like a hat, in Djemma elFna. All the bustle and weirdness of the square was much less intimidating than Liz had imagined. I have to keep reminding myself of its strangeness.

The next evening we had our first Santa sighting - little plastic blow-up toys -we must buy one to join Osama.

I took Liz to the Jardin Majorelle very early the next morning where she was suitably impressed. Luckily the throngs of English garden ladies from the Home Counties had yet to arrive with their shrieks of delight at the plantings and, "Oh, Marjorie, *do* look at the geraniums!"

In the afternoon Peter, Liz and I went out sightseeing leaving Robert to paint in peace. When we got back Liz went upstairs to get some thing or other and discovered that she couldn't find her camera…or her phone… or the handbag with her passport in it, and we realized we had been robbed. Peter and Liz, the last ones on the roof, hadn't shut the security door thinking it was all right to leave it open when Robert was to stay behind.

Someone must have snuck in incredibly quietly while Robert was engrossed in his painting and rushed to the bedroom, snatched whatever he could, and escaped up the stairs to the roof.

The police were summoned by Ismail and the items stolen detailed. Since the things stolen belonged to Liz, she and I and Ghislan and the police officers processed to the police station by Bab Aylen where a large number of forms were filled out by hand in triplicate. Apparently the police department did, briefly, have computers which vanished almost immediately.

Liz's name?
Elizabeth Wix
My name
Elizbeth Wix Schmid
Liz's mother's name?
Judy Haire
My husband's name
Robert Schmid
Did my brother have two wives?
No.
Why have my brother's wife and his sister got the same name?

And so on.

I told Ghislan to phone her mother to say she would be late getting home.

I was dying to pee.

Not possible. Toilet much too filthy for madame.

Desperate. Yes, the toilet was filthy. The kind where you plant your feet above the abyss and hope not to fall in.

The details were finally recorded. Night fell and it was time for everyone to go home, but throngs of other people were heading home too. There was a great bustle in the street and we were a long way from derb Djedid. Ghislan hailed a caleche with jingling harness bells and I told her that it was the first time I've been in one. "Don't they have them in your city?" she asked. She negotiated an amazingly cheap price and we rode home through the night town and it felt as if Christmas was coming and I got the idea for a children's story set in England.

Both Peter and Liz were remarkably calm about the whole robbery and well prepared with duplicate documents and insurance plans. We eventually got a paper allowing Liz to leave the country from the British Consulate in Gueliz.

November 23, 2006

Judy Flaherty called and invited me to visit the American School; she also asked me if I would be remotely interested in doing a two week substitute teaching assignment just before Christmas. I said yes to both - since two weeks is not such a long time and I was interested to see the school.

I had to get up early to get up to pick up the American school bus in Gueliz. Robert's expensive orange and green plastic alarm clock had let us down and I ended up in a great rush with no packed lunch. The school is about six miles from the city in a big spacious airy campus with modern buildings on the route to Ouzzazzate.

The kindergarten children were charming and the day busy and well organized. I observed Mrs. El Harti's class since she was going back to America for two weeks. The children were rehearsing their end of term entertainment "If you're happy and you know it…" Luckily, at that age, if they do it wrong, everyone thinks it is cute rather than disastrous.

All the instruction is in English and we have to discourage side-chat in Arabic or French. One little Italian boy, Matteo, cried his eyes out because Mrs. ElHarti didn't like that he colored his picture all blue. He recovered quite quickly. The art project was gluing colored feathers onto a footprint which turned into a turkey.

The head teacher of the lower school, Audrey Riffi, whom I chatted to at lunch, is English - a doctor's daughter from Essex who has lived in Morocco for many years and knew Paul Bowles in Tangiers. I agreed to do the brief teaching stint.

Mrs. El Harti, whose Anglo name is Monte Atwell, and I got a ride back into town with a parent at the end of the afternoon. Monte lives pretty near us in the medina and was a medical technician in Florida in her other life. She has no early education credentials at all.

In the evening we walked into the souks where an entire building has collapsed. A huge heap of tumbled mud brick with a chandelier swinging from a ceiling. We were told not to take photographs of it.

Because we had Peter and Liz staying, we really hadn't made plans for, or organized anything for Thanksgiving.

Two days before we had received a piece of paper from Maroc Poste through the front door, but, since it was all in Arabic, we didn't know it meant.

After seeing Pete and Liz off at the airport, I went to the post office in Djmma elFna to send off our son's fiancee's Christmas present - a predictably long and complicated proceeding. I sat in a large green painted back room while a man produced a box and numerous documents. After the package was finally dispatched, I showed them the paper which had come through the door and they said yes, it was a package but at the main post office in Gueliz not there in the medina.

On Thanksgiving morning, I went on the bus to the Poste in Gueliz and showed the paper and, after shuffling about in the back room for a while, they produced an interesting looking package addressed to Robert Schmid. I showed my NY driver's license to show I was SCHMID but they asked for Robert's passport. No, they couldn't possibly give the parcel to me. They needed *mon mari* in person. I was in a fury having seen the package but not being allowed to have it, so rushed home. Robert and I plus passport went back on the bus to the PO again.

The package was from Jennifer and Garret and said on the contents:
STUFFING and CRANBERRY SAUCE.

Great joy and excitement. On the way home we bought some turkey breast from the *bibi* butcher on Dabachi. Then I said, "But what are we going to do for gravy?" and Robert said, "Perhaps when you fry the turkey there will be some juices."

When we arrived home there was a knock on the door with someone wanting our details as *etrangers* living in the neighborhood. We are never quite sure whether these inquisitive people are sent by some sort of local governmental agency or merely want to see the inside of our house. Eventually the man departed, and we opened our package to see: Stovetop Stuffing, a can of Oceanspray Cranberry Jelly and …two packets of gravy mix. American Thanksgiving in a box.

So we went off and bought roses to decorate the table, cooked peas and mashed potato and had a fine Thanksgiving feast. After which we went dead asleep thinking how wonderfully kind it was of Jennifer and Garret to think of us.

November 26, 2006

Young Moroccans love clothing with designer logos. A recent sighting on the bus: a sweatshirt with
FBI
Federal Bureac of InYestigation
written on the back.

Yesterday Loobna, the receptionist from Hotel Sherazade, and Ghislan came to tea. We had to sit in the salon as it was pouring with rain. I had expected them on Sunday at four and this was Saturday at three so sent Robert rushing off in the downpour to procure cake. He bought little tiny pastries with nuts and honey.

Both young women approved of Robert's Malika el Marakshia CD - bought in Djemma el Fna. Robert said he thought it sounded a little Egyptian but they insisted it was pure Marrakech.

Today it's amazingly clear and you can see every little detail of the mountains. It has turned much cooler and the roof is OK to sit on in the sun for more than five minutes. We replaced a failing trumpet vine with a small mauve bougenvillia.

While sitting on the roof enjoying the autumnal sunshine, we noticed several Moroccans wearing leather jackets posted on various roof tops nearby. They indicated to us to sit down, but not before we had caught a glimpse of a slight, djellaba-clad man hopping desperately from roof top to roof top. Then the leather jacketed police officers closed in on him.

We heard much clapping from the derb and ran down and opened our front door to see what was going on. Everyone else was looking out too, including Mustafa, our potion seller friend, as the little thief was led away handcuffed between two burly officers. Apparently there had been quite a lot of robberies lately and this was the culprit.

The robber was a pathetic figure, small, pale and ragged - probably in from the countryside and penniless. We asked Ismail what would happen to him and he said the robber would get seven years in jail at least. When we said that seemed rather a long time, Ismail shrugged and said he was a thief - what did he expect?

The next morning we heard that Mustafa the potion seller is dead - a horrible surprise since he appeared so strong and healthy the previous day and his children are so young.

"Ismail, how can he possibly be dead? What happened? Was it an accident? His heart?"

Ismail merely said, "From God."

"Yes, of course, from God. But how? There must have been some reason."

Ismail merely shook his head and we never found out anything more. We saw the potion seller's widow for the first time as she emerged all clad in white from her house with her daughter. She looked very young - possibly in her early twenties - and had a beautiful smile which transformed her pale face.

One afternoon soon after this a young boy arrived at the door with a message from the police in the medina. I was to go to the police station in Djemma Elfna to describe exactly what was stolen since some things have been recovered. At the police station I meet a fellow riad owner who bemoaned the loss of an expensive belt that belonged to his wife. I really am not too worried about the things that Liz lost because most can be replaced and are covered by insurance anyway.

The next day two policeman arrived at our house with the pathetic little thief between them. They asked the thief to agree that this was where he had stolen from - though I don't believe he was ever in the courtyard. My main feeling was pity for him. I avoided meeting his eyes.

December

On Tuesday we went to Marjane to look for plant food and see if they had any Christmas decorations - things not to be had in the medina. We found the plant food - Liz had said the pots on the roof needed minerals because the dirt was such poor quality. We bought a knife for chopping things - having survived since August with one tiny paring knife. I bought a little packet of Malteesers too.

The Christmas decorations were billed as *"Fin de Annee"* and there were shiny balls and tinsel and artificial trees. We didn't buy anything except a small tin of Quality Street chocolates to be hidden for later on - it's not that I really like Quality Street - it's just that the tin was exactly the same as it was in the 1950's and I can remember all the different shapes of chocolates inside.

Robert bought a plastic ruler and then, as we stood together at the checkout, we both looked at the gleaming golden arches of MacDonald's. It was way past lunch time. I said, "Would it be so very awful if…?"

So Robert had a Burger Supreme and I had Fillet O'Fish and we both had fries and the grease tasted wonderful.

We have been watching movies on the computer - Monte gets them pirated somewhere in the souks. We see whatever is available - not our choices exactly, however the first movies or TV we've seen since August. We saw Prime - all set in New York and it didn't make me miss it at all. Other than that it was psychopaths week: Ed Harris doing a good party turn in something with Sean Connery, and Morgan Freeman quite wasted in Kiss the Girls.

Then Harrison Ford being tough and threatened in Firewall. Obligatory car chases and explosions. Robert had been reading Boccaccio every evening - so this made a change.

We have been talking about time travel and how it is used as a plot device in literature. Here some of the caleches have bells on, like the one we came back from the police station in, and jingle down the lanes carrying people home from work or shopping. Some of the drivers wear the pointed hooded djellabahs which makes the whole thing look like one of the illustrations in *The Lion the Witch and the Wardrobe*. The small donkeys are so placid and long suffering -almost Biblical. The Atlas Mountains - so clearly visible now with the snow on the top of them - make me think of Eliot's *Journey of the Magi*. Too many literary allusions - probably a good thing I'm going to teach four year olds next week.

Mimi the slim little cat has reappeared and I'm spoiling her with Heinz tuna. We really enjoy having a cat to play with. Mimi, however, having finished her tuna, would prefer to stalk the sparrows.

Ismail is going to ask his father about getting us a real Christmas tree. Preferably one in a pot with roots which can later go up on the terrace.

December 3, 2006

Instead of being woken up by the birds demanding food, we are now woken by Mimi who sticks her head over the parapet and looks down on us. The birds do not like this at all. She has a most insistent howl.

Yesterday was the first day of the International film festival. They have put a giant screen in the main square but there are other venues as well. We got tickets for *Mediterraneo* - an old Italian movie - with French subtitles. As we walked across

Djemma elFna to get to the bus stop, it came on to rain and was altogether wintry and we were glad to arrive at Cinema Collesseo on Boulevard Zerktouni which was clean and comfortable although pitch dark. Whenever there was anything remotely sexy on the screen, there were wolf whistles and cheers from the mostly young audience.

Brad Pitt and Susan Sarandon are meant to be in town, but, needless to say, we have not seen them.

We had supper at Charly's Cabana and were glad of the warmth from the pizza oven. Winter seems to be upon us.

On Friday on rue Dabachi I saw a man, obviously from the country, looking after two sheep. Yesterday I saw a ram with big curling horns being driven on a moped down Boulevard Mohammed V. Loobna told us that on Eid Kabir, which this year falls on New Year's Eve, a sheep is slaughtered in every home to commemorate Abraham's attempted sacrifice of Isaac or Ibrahim's attempted sacrifice of Ismael. I'm not sure I'm looking forward to this.

Mimi has almost moved in. She sleeps under the covers when we take a nap. She has also taken to inviting a fluffy black and white tomcat to visit her on the roof. He also gazes at us from the parapet and demands food.

The latest cat snacks are chicken heads. A cat in Djemma elFna was sitting guarding hers - gazing transfixed at it as if the rest of the chicken might magically appear.

Ismail is going to chef school. He is also going to arrange for two more shelves for me in the alcove in my study. He says they should be angled like a step pyramid for *decor*. I like my monk's cell-like study very much with its big table which faces the metal-grille window to the courtyard. I manage to get quite a lot of writing done despite the constant interruptions from people coming to the front door. For some reason - possibly damp - I avoid the end of the room that abuts the religious people's. Whether this is out of politeness towards them or because that end has a kind of aura I can never be quite certain. We have not heard any more from Ismail about the Christmas tree.

A very pale mule has been gussied up to look prettier - it was quite covered in henna blotches which had worn off where the harness was.

Because it is 45F at night and raining, we went to Marjane and bought two heaters. One has a propane tank and Ismail said if we slept with it on we would end up *mut*. The salon now gets toasty warm in five minutes but we have to be certain to leave the salon doors partially open to avoid being asphyxiated. Then we have to run up to the bedroom very quickly and leap into bed. In the mornings we turn on the electric fan heater for a few minutes so it gets warm enough to get dressed. The Moroccans tend to warm the person adding layers of clothing rather than warming rooms.

December 10, 2006

My first day of teaching. Derb Djedid is deserted at seven in the morning but people walk purposefully through the cold morning air on derb Dabachi. The bakeries are open and it's possible to buy a warm *pain chocolat*. A street vendor is dishing out what looks like gruel from a large metal container near Cafe France. People wear the hoods of their djellabas up.

I get a cab up to Hotel Kabir on Boulevard Zerktouni, past the empty, misty Cyber Park and the Katoubia. There is little traffic. Here I pick up the bus. Except for not being yellow, it is an American school bus - Bluebird brand - but here for teachers and assistants not students who are all delivered to school by parents or drivers.

    Judy greets me and others nod and smile. The ride lasts about twenty minutes and goes out on the route de Ouazzazate towards the Atlas through the outskirts of town, and out into the country. As the sun comes up, the palm trees loom out of the mist. Near the school campus there are vast unfinished mansions with views of the Atlas Mountains.

    The four year olds are charming, exasperating and wiggly as worms - just like four year olds anywhere - except these children already speak French and Arabic and English will be their third language.

    They call me Mrs.Witch because they can't say Wix. I rather like it.

    The teachers are expatriates from England, Ireland and America. Many have been here for years and I look forward to discovering their various stories. I have two teaching assistants, both willing and conscientious. Unfortunately Mr. Abdellatif, in the Moroccan style, keeps order by shouting at the children - something I think should be kept for a last resort. I try to model calm even though Abelkader, the wiggliest and youngest of the children, could drive one quite mad.

    The children have two long playtimes in the large gravel covered garden and when they fall down and cry it is quite usual to take them on your knee and kiss them better. Much more natural than being frightened to touch anyone.

    In the afternoon when we make Christmas trees with glitter and sequins, I do not tell the children not to put the sequins in their mouths because I think it might give some of the more adventurous of them ideas. Luckily no one does.

    The teachers eat lunch at picnic tables on the roof in the warm sun and discuss all things Moroccan. Apparently the hotels are upset that Eid and New Year's fall on the same day - usually they get two sets of holidays and therefore two sets of guests.

Anyway, I'm told a sheep is slaughtered in every house - the butcher comes round to do it if no male family member is available - and there is blood everywhere. The sheep is devoured in a sequence of organs beginning - so far as I can discover - by kidney and liver brochettes. A soup is made from the brains.

December 15, 2006

The performance by the four year olds went off without any major disasters though at the dress rehearsal Carla peed in her pants. On the big day only three children cried and the over-enthusiastic parents were more troublesome than the kids. The whole thing was videoed multiple times. There was a towering Christmas tree festooned with ornaments. Santa, aka the Arabic teacher, arrived and gave out bags of candy assisted by Judy Flaherty dressed up as *Mere Noel*. The tinies were almost stampeded in the crush of very large 5th graders rushing up to claim their goodies. Mrs. Riffi played the piano.

Altogether a busy week. At Monday's book club we sat in as American a house as you can get in Morocco. There was lots of tile and cut plaster work but all the muddled artifacts of American middle class life too - the Christmas tree and family photos from Sears. Lots of good food including Cadbury's chocolate fingers. It was pretty chilly but there was hot soup. We discussed *The Namesake* which led to long discussions on English and Arabic names. Sarah's husband, from an English Jewish family, is now Muslim and called Yehyeh - having grown up as John. Sayeed means happy - Felix in English, Sayeeda, Felicia. Ghislan means a herd of little deer. Noor means beautiful night.

On Tuesday we had Caitlin and Samuel, Americans we had met at Tahir Shah's reading, to supper. We ate in my study, heated by the gas fire instead of sitting in the courtyard. In place of a table cloth, Robert had painted a large paper with a design based on a Berber design found on the Mouassine fountain. I had thought of putting a white scarf on the table but Robert thought it would get wrecked. We had ordered one of Ismail's mother's tagines.

In the early evening Ismail arrived and set the table with salads and bread, and when we were ready to eat, Ismail appeared with the steaming dish and uncovered it with his usual theatrical flourish. Then we discovered the cork screw was missing and Caitlin and I went to a nearby maison d'hotes to ask to borrow theirs. A corkscrew is called a *tire bouchon*, I discovered.

The Koran forbids the consumption of alcohol and it's not possible to buy it in the medina - though the disreputable Hotel Tazi serves beer. So we often go up to Gueliz and buy Carlsburg and wine which is then hidden in non see-through bags and smuggled home. Samuel suggests that one of the bicycles that deliver "*Mediciments Urgents*" could be co-opted as a discreet delivery service for alcohol seekers in the medina.

In addition to the book group, the ex-pats have a wine tasting club which attracts rather the same people minus those women married to Moroccans who don't approve of alcohol or their wives socializing with men outside of the family. On Thursday I went to my first wine tasting. On the way there Judy and I were in a taxi that was cut off by a big black SUV and got into a fender bender - no one was hurt - we merely got out and got in another taxi leaving the furious drivers to fight it out.

Mary Mimouna, who is married to a non-disapproving Moroccan, hosted the event and took it very seriously and had pencil and paper at the ready to take notes. At first we were only allowed to sniff the wine, then to sip it - and at last take a full mouthful. There were four wines with the labels covered up to prevent us from cheating. Two wines were French and two were Moroccan and none really interesting to my undiscerning palate but the chicken liver pate served as a side dish was delicious.

I got home to discover Robert watching Monte's pirated DVD's sitting up in bed with the electric heater on and told him he could go to the next tasting since there were men there.

December 16, 2006

Ismail's father didn't seem to have located a Christmas tree and there were none at the plant place in Djemma elFna - only a few rather over grown poinsettias. There were some cut evergreens outside the Marche Centrale in Gueliz but no real firs so I decided to go to Metro - a huge warehouse store where people who run bed and breakfasts go to buy in bulk. It is out on the route to Fez, almost as far as the American school and I went by taxi.

There the trees were real firs - of the rather scraggy, skinny English variety which I like. Also these were *avec racine* which I had some dim memory meant root. The tree was put in the trunk of the taxi which took me back to Cafe France and a man with a cart brought it to derb Djedid. I had told the taxi man it was *'pour la terrasse'* in case he was against Christmas.

Mary Mimouna had a maid who for five years quite happily accepted Christmas presents - a set of Koranic books one year, a pair of shoes another - but then decided she could no longer have anything whatsoever to do with the holiday. She had been given tracts from by a Wahhabi friend and was becoming more and more strictly observant - she could no longer clear the table if there were wine glasses on it. She needed more time off to pray. She needed to wear her headscarf indoors in case a man glimpsed her from the street as she worked. Soon her religious observations consumed so much of her time that there was scarcely any left for anything else. Finally Mary spoke to her. Was it worth risking her job? Yes, better to live in poverty than burn in hell.

Robert was most impressed with the scrawny Christmas tree and we watered it and placed it in the courtyard to await decorations. Ismail was also thrilled with it and wanted to know about Mary and Joseph and baby Jesus. So I went to the supermarket in Gueliz and bought some chocolate ornaments and some glitter glue to make paper decorations.

There are no Christmas cards as such here but little French New Year's cards with robins and glitter on. When I went to the post office to buy stamps I said the cards were so pretty - better than in America and the man said surely not - so I had to agree they were merely different.

I addressed the cards sitting outside at Cafe France thinking it was very pleasant to be outside in the middle of December.

December 19, 2006

Walking down scruffy old Dabachi, all freighted with shopping, I noticed some paintings on the ground amidst the pirated CD's and cheap wooly leggings. They were pictures of animals and landscapes painted on hardboard with industrial paints. There are a bull, a leopard, a dusky maiden up a tree - but the one I liked most is of mosque in the desert with a palm tree. There was also one of a circus horse and a bird with a mosque, in quite different proportions, in the lower left. They are magical, if a little batty.

The unprosperous-looking artist was charming and eager to sell me all he had. I offered him about ten dollars for two paintings and he seemed thrilled and wanted to sell me the rest too. I have rarely bought a painting since we make them at home.

Robert liked the pictures too and we looked at the artist's other paintings again as we walked to cafe France. The next day I went back and asked if he would paint me a picture of a chicken. He asked how many chickens and I said two. He said they will be ready the next morning .

When I rushed out to Dabachi the next day I couldn't find the painter.

After lunch Robert found a different man with the paintings but not the actual painter who "had to go back to his home place". I asked when he would be back. The left-over paintings were rather sad and brownish blue. In a disconsolate sort of way, the man offers us all of them for two dollars. Perhaps one day my picture of chickens will appear.

Houses

One of the pleasures of living in Morocco is visiting other people's houses to see how they have decided to interpret the delights and challenges of restoring old buildings in the medina. Obviously most of our friends are ex-patriates and come from countries where houses are designed quite differently. Here most houses have few, if any, exterior windows and center round a courtyard - from the street it's impossible to tell what each door will reveal. When most of the houses were built there was little in the way of plumbing - usually just one cold tap. Baths were taken at the hammam and the toilet was often situated just near the front door so there was just a short distance to the sewers. One of the things Europeans do is to add bathrooms and showers aplenty which puts a great strain on the antiquated sewer system.

One of the most miserable jobs in the medina must be working on problems in the drains - something that happens pretty often. The drain cover is opened and the wretched worker, in gum boots, descends to see what's up. This job is often done by rather slight men who fit down the drain hole - it reminds me how child chimney sweepers were used in the 19th century in Europe - employed simply because their bodies fit the space.

Apart from the plumbing, heating and cooling present challenges. Not much air-conditioning and no central heating. The basic design of the houses lends itself well to the climate - for most of the year the courtyards act as extended living rooms - cool in the summer and somewhat protected in the winter. When it gets very cold a single room can be heated.

Anyway, after the basics are taken care of, the next thoughts are of color and texture. The floors are always tiled - therefore easy to wash down - and of many and various designs - black and white checkered is very popular - though there is a delicious amount of choice. No fitted carpets here - though throw rugs abound. The walls are plastered and either painted or done in *tadelkt* - a rather lovely polished plaster. Sometimes there is decorative cut plaster work forming bands round the walls. The doors are always of wood often painted with complex designs. Ours are a rather too bright red which Robert improved with a darker varnish to diminish the rather fairground look.

December 20, 2006

I was walking by the laundry when I saw a pleasant looking, plump man with a donkey cart. The donkey was so charming I stopped to rub his nose.

The man said, "I call that one Mr. Blair."

"But surely your donkey is nicer?" I said.

Much laughter.

"He smarter," the man said.

Another pretty grey donkey emerged from the ally.

"That one Mr. Bush. Him smarter than Mr. Bush too."

These two were rather unusual - most donkeys don't have names at all.

December 23, 2006

Claudia was due to arrive at 12:35am on Saturday morning, but after being delayed by fog at Gatwick, she arrived at Marrakech airport at 4:18am aboard a "Smartwings" plane. It was Czech and still had ashtrays in the arm rests. Apparently the woman sitting next to her had had panic attacks the whole flight.

We had got up at four and walked through Djemma el Fna which was almost totally deserted - probably six people in the entire square - an unusual experience. Claudia brought lots of presents with her including a hot water bottle from Rosie - an excellent choice of present when the nights were very cold. She had also managed to smuggle some frozen Wall's pork chipolata sausages.

On Christmas Eve Claudia and I went to a little carol service at the Protestant Hall in the grounds of the Catholic church. It was exactly like a church hall anywhere - rather barren but with tinsel decorations and a Christmas tree and cookies and snacks as you'd find in England and America. The children lit candles on the Advent wreath and acted a short play. A soldier and a policeman were posted by the gates. I had worried a little about asking the taxi driver to take us to the church but was assured that it was better to be perceived as Christian than without a religion at all - a stance quite shocking to most Moroccans.

In the afternoon we wrapped presents and wrote messages in glitter glue. We had dinner at Cafe Arabe where Christmas songs - instead of the usual Michael Jackson or opera - were played. There was a pretty rose and holly decoration on the table and a real fir tree with lots of silver glitter. On the way home, outside Bis 23, the little hanut, we were greeted by one of our neighbors, Sayeed, and Robert said -in Arabic - that tomorrow was Christmas and Sayeed wished us a *"Joyeaux Noel"*.

Claudia is much taken with Mimi who sidled up to her as she sunbathed on the roof. Mimi is now allowed into the house all the time.

On Christmas Day we feasted on turkey and the smuggled sausages and sat in the little salon with the fire on and the door cracked open. Then we ate all the Lindt airport chocolate Claudia had brought with her.

December 28, 2006

"HowAreYou" lives the other end of derb Djedid just near Riad Noga. He sits in his doorway and greets us whenever we pass by. His usual greeting is "How are you?" and then we progress to *"L'bas"* and *" Bechir Al'hamdu'llah'* and so forth. He is probably forty years old - he has introduced us to his aged father. Sometimes he is in exuberantly good spirits and sometimes he is so downcast he can scarcely nod. We wonder whether he is, perhaps, a little simple; anyway, he is a constant presence in the neighborhood. He often cadges cigarettes for which he seems very grateful.

Shortly after Christmas, on my way to the laundry, I saw a small van parked outside "Howareyou"'s house and a little crowd gathered all looking pretty cheerful.

They indicated I should look into the house as a *'manteau'* - I misheard - they meant *'mouton'* was being pushed upstairs - there it was: a sheep's rear-end with two people shoving it upwards. Even the women seemed very welcoming. The sheep will spend the next four days being petted and eating hay on the roof and then, on Sunday, it will proceed directly to heaven and all its bits and bobs will be eaten. We discover that HowAreYou's real name is Abdjelli.

The medina is full of people and sheep crammed into the backs of vans and little boys selling hay and oats for the sheep. The general feeling is festive.

January 2007

On the morning of Eid Kabir all the little local shops were closed. On Dabachi I saw a ram being taken out of the trunk of a large Mercedes and having its last picture taken on a cell phone.

About eleven we decided to take a walk and groups of young men in their best clothes were hovering expectantly in doorways.

In Dabachi Square there were blazing bonfires of charcoal and old boards - with rams' heads blackening in the flames and a smell of burning wool.

There was no bread to be had in the whole town. We walked up past the mellah and all down rue Riad Zitoun Djedid asking where we could find some bread. We saw a young man on his way back from the bakery who kindly offered us some fresh homemade bread - but I refused it because his mother might have been furious if he arrived home without it.

Abdjelli was sitting in his doorway and invited us in to see the current state of his *mouton*. We climbed the steep stairs to see the clean carcass hanging from the ceremonial hook in the small upstairs kitchen. His mother looked very happy and proud. We offered Season's Greetings and *Mezyan Eid*.

On both sides of our house smoke rose from barbeques and sheepskins dried on roofs.

In the afternoon Ismail arrived with two lamb's liver kebabs in pita bread - and a movie on his cellphone of the killing of the sacrificial ram. I didn't look at the video but Robert said Ismail's grandfather had slit the throat quickly and it was all over in seconds - no sound or struggle.

I ate my kebab with a little salt on while Robert tried, and failed, to hook up Ismail's phone via Bluetooth to the computer - so we could make a DVD of the sacrifice for Ismail. We will try again soon. I have hidden Robert's kebabs in the fridge since he couldn't face eating them any more than I could see pictures of the ram's demise.

We had supper at David H's house to celebrate the New Year. He had a house party of rather elderly 1960's people - of the *Absolutely Fabulous* variety -who insisted David should provide *kif* to accompany the champagne and oysters. Poor David had been sent out to procure the said item - and succeeded. We never asked exactly how or where since as residents who everyone knows pretty much everything about, it is better to keep a low profile. *Kif* smoked, champagne drunk, his guests passed out on the banquettes. We decided that we all, as English and American people, are culturally illiterate in Morocco - however long one has lived here.

We walked home through Djemma elFna just before one. People were still eating at darkened stalls. We had missed the New Year's fireworks. David had told us to watch out for drunken Moroccans, who, unfamiliar with alcohol, don't behave very well. We didn't meet any.

For Christmas Robert and I had given each other totally untransportable items - I gave him a huge mirror surrounded by a checkerboard of black and white camel bone and he gave me a delicate green glass vase both of us had admired in Gueliz in October. The mirror was precariously hung in the hall - in the Moroccan style where it tilts slightly forward and appears just about to fall off and kill somebody. It looks very spiffy. We take these untransportable gifts as signs we will stay in Morocco.

January brought our wedding anniversary and both our birthdays so we decided to buy a chest for the hall. We wandered Bab Khemis, the large second hand market where you can buy used furniture, new furniture, ceramic pots, electronic goods, shoes, carpets and planks of wood and everything else you can imagine. Currently there is a mass of the ex-contents of La Mamounia which is being refurbished. While I was admiring a very charming pointer puppy, Robert smashed a decorated plate - quite by accident. He had been trying the drawer of a pretty, small black chest of drawers. The man refused payment for the plate; the chest was charming, so we bought it.

The shop owner summoned a little truck to haul the chest home. We wondered how much this transport would cost - in the end $8. Robert and the chest were installed on the back of the truck while I rode in the front. It was quite a feat getting out of the crowded market. When I thought we were quite blocked in, the driver hopped out and he and another man physically pushed aside a parked truck.

The ride home seemed unending and I was sure Robert would be asphyxiated by all the moped fumes. At one point the horse from the caleche following us put his head inside the truck to look at me. We drove down derb Dabachi and our friend Mustafa the cigarette salesman helped us carry the chest home where it now graces the hall beneath camel bone mirror.

Later that day we were walking down rue Riad Zitoune L'Kedim on our way to the Mellah when Robert, who was looking quite scruffy, was struck by a desire to have a shave and haircut. Neima, the barber, has a very small shop all in shades of brown, and a certificate attesting to his barbering skills, probably from the 70's, framed on the wall.

Neima's chair was large and imposing and first he washed Robert's hair - having doused the straight razor with alcohol and set it alight. I sat and looked at the two magazines - one from Janvier 2001 and the other a sort of TV guide from Ramadan 2002. Neima did a very thorough job including blow dryer and hairspray; he shaved Robert twice and gave him a face massage with argan cream. I was quite jealous. All this took a very long time and so we didn't get to the mellah because we had to get back because Monte was coming to tea. Monte brought her little dog which barked at Mimi who threatened to slice the little Pekinese to pieces - we were quite proud of Mimi - you do not mess with Moroccan alley cats.

Snippets:

Lots of the dingier men-only cafes are named for cold things - so far our collection includes The Snowball, Igloo, Arctic, Iceberg and Glacier.

We cannot walk anywhere without meeting someone we know - yesterday it was Hassan a waiter from Sherazade. We stop and shake hands or kiss.

While we were having tea on our roof, a man called to Robert from the roof of bis 115 - the other half of our house - and asked Robert if we wanted to buy it. The man said we would then have a big house and could turn it into a bed and breakfast.

We have to contact the man - who seemed to be some sort of real estate agent - at his office to find out the price, but we do not want to run a bed and breakfast. But we might be about to become a hostel for kittens. No sooner had Claudia returned to England, having thoroughly adopted Mimi and given her the run of the house, than it became obvious that Mimi was no longer the sleek young virgin we had first encountered.

Roger, who lived next door to me in England when I was growing up, is visiting from London so we are doing the sights. We visit the square in the evening with new eyes. Robert likes the lute player.

We think Roger should see the countryside and since we don't have a car decide to risk a little mini-bus tour suggested by the tourist office in Gueliz. There are eight people on the trip plus a guide and a driver. We go first to Asni where we could see Mt. Toubkal in the distance - one of the highest peaks in Africa. Then we took the Ourika Valley though farmland reminiscent of Italy and stopped for mint tea in a mud-brick Berber family house, complete with two cows indoors and friendly women laughing merrily.

Then we drove for about an hour on fairly precipitous roads - but not nearly as scary as the High Atlas. There were groves of apples, olives, and almonds - often on steep land that had been terraced into the hillside. To reach the other side of the river from the road you had to walk across handmade board bridges supported by cables. How on earth would you get a refrigerator or sofa over there? Perhaps you're just plain out of luck.

When we reached Setti Fatma - the end of the road - we started walking along the river bank on a stony mud path with big boulders. The only way to travel was by foot or on a donkey. It didn't take long to get away from civilization - bright blue sky, no pollution, and - *alhamdilillah* - no mopeds. We walked for about two or three miles until we found ourselves alone in the mountains in the steep-sided valley beside the raging, snow fed river. I ended up paddling in the stream rather than hopping from boulder to boulder - safer to get my feet wet than fall in completely. There are meant to be wild boars about there there but we didn't see any.

Walking back, I made Robert take photographs of various very free-range chickens. A woman was tending goats with her baby strapped to her back. I wondered whether she had ever been out of her village; her life and surroundings seemed timeless.

We bought olive oil from an oil press where we had to provide a plastic bottle to put it in - about a litre of virgin oil for fifty cents.

February

We were in England for nine days seeing family and getting a very small taste of English winter. There was a light, picturesque dusting of snow our first morning and a freezing wind as we walked with Claudia round Spitalfields and went out for a pub lunch. After that it was pretty mild with spring flowers much more advanced than they should be.

Robert and I have discovered that we are getting rather bad at being away from our simple, pleasantly dull routine in Marrakesh and were happy to be welcomed back by Ismail who had looked after Mimi very well. He had a toothache and I don't envy him going to a dentist here. We plied him with Advil which helped a little.

The weather in Marrakesh is overcast and rainy which must be a blessing for the farmers since there hadn't been any rain since November.

In addition to roses there are now lots of blue irises in the market.

Our second night home was Ashura a festival which entailed young men beating drums and singing from 10pm until 12:30 right outside our front door. It was not very tuneful and, when I could stand it no longer, I poked my head outside the door and smiled weakly - they smiled back probably thinking I was enjoying the drumming as much as they were. It eventually ended.

Mimi is absurdly fat.

All in all, we were glad to be home.

February 16, 2007

It was 83F yesterday and miserably hot on the ALSA bus. The tourists have all busted out their shorts, and Robert has retrieved his flip-flops from wherever they were hiding. The flower sellers have more and more of the beautiful blue irises. Spring has sprung.

Monday was book club and Malin produced a veritable feast - turkey stuffed into pita bread, mini pizzas, harira soup and amazing blondies. I am a little worried that when it is my turn next month I will have rather a lot to keep up with.

Because of book club, I have had a stupid week. Having foolishly chosen Sarah Waters' *Night Watch* - a super read but five hundred pages, I was left with the problem of making copies. I went to a copy place in Gueliz on Monday with the book and ordered eight sets which would be ready on Tuesday.

I went there on Tuesday and they weren't ready. They said the day after tomorrow - Thursday. The copy shop people were all excited when I arrived and handed me a stack of 2,500 uncollated pages. A daunting task. I then spent two hours collating them, noticing as I went what a horrible job they had made of the copying. Pages not fully visible, pages upside down, pages too pale. Thumb prints were the least of it. Had it been at Staples in New York, I would simply have refused to take such a lousy job, but having seen the poor man at work at it, and thinking of all the trees, paper and ink, like a fool, I accepted it. They said they would give me the bindings for free. Then, of course they hadn't done the bindings and I had to send poor Judy in to collect this mess. There were so many errors we had to abandon the whole project and read short stories available on line instead. In future we want to order real books because at least then you can keep them and it doesn't violate copyright. It's just that you have to plan ahead.

Walking the back way to rue Riad Zitoune L'kadim and the Maison Tiskiwin with Roger we noticed a a rather bashed up, fierce looking gray mother cat with four little kittens in a cardboard box. The kittens were tiny and still had the dried-up umbilical cords attached. The one I liked best was gray and white. The mother cat had a bowl of milk beside her and some rather sun-dried liver.

Mimi is getting bigger and bigger and upset us the other day when she disappeared for almost twenty four hours. We thought she had gone out to have her kittens elsewhere, but no, she reappeared, fatter than ever, and as of now is reclining in state in the middle of our bed.

Maison Tiskwin, Bert Flint's museum of Saharan and SubSaharan artifacts is fascinating in a jumbled, Pitt-Rivers sort of way. It is housed in two adjoining riads and full of pottery, fabrics, jewelry, metal work and elaborate basketry. The robes all had the same basic designs on, swirls of embroidery to represent the sun. Robert spent ages copying designs when he found his camera battery had suddenly died, and said somehow they echoed cellular automatrons. What it made me think more than anything was how very hard the people's lives were who lived amongst all this. How heavy the jewelry and how unwieldy to wear.

We had met Bert Flint in the summer, on the boiling hot day when we last went there. He is very old and distinguished, but, sadly, quite deaf so it was hard to have a conversation. There is a map of where all the various tribes whose names are evocative and lovely. It makes me want to go and look at Dogon castles and one day visit Timbuctoo, which I had thought until recently was a made-up place.

February 19, 2007

    This morning I went to Marjane where last week they said they would have the mustard that Robert likes - the kind with seeds in *"A la Ancienne"*. When I got to the mustard shelf it was exactly as it was before - lots and lots of other mustard but a big gap where this particular type should be.

    I broke down and bought kitty litter since I do not want fat Mimi to have her kittens in some dim hole where we won't have the pleasure of seeing them. Bought beer and paper towels - the usual sort of boring stuff that you can't get in the medina and ended up needing a cart man from outside Cafe France to haul the stuff home. Cart man etiquette is rather complicated. Their income from transporting packages is small and I wish I could hire all of them. I try to chose a man I recognize since he will know where I live, and be insulted if I chose a new person. I couldn't see anyone I immediately recognized and nodded to the group by the mosque. A man I didn't know loaded up the cart rushed energetically down derb Dabachi - when we got home I said he could put the stuff by the front door and tipped him, but he dashed into the courtyard and put the bags on the table - and helped himself to a banana.

February 20, 2007

    After getting so huge we thought she would explode and keeping us waiting for a very long time, Mimi had five kittens last night in the cupboard in the salon where we had made a nest for her. One black, one black and white, two black, orange and white, and one who looks remarkably like one of Mimi's stupider boyfriends - the one with the dim expression who threw up behind the palm tree the first time we saw him. They all look like little shut-eyed hamsters but are charming to watch. Because it is pouring with rain, the whole gang spent the day in the salon with the heater on. My quilt will have to be abandoned.

This afternoon there was a thunderstorm which is quite unusual here and we got soaking wet and covered in mud and slop on derb Dabachi. In the evening we wanted to watch pirated DVD's on the computer in bed - well, we would watch un-pirated DVD's if they were available. Four out of the five we bought, having been told they were in English, turned out to be in French, and, since they weren't wonderful movies in the first place, it seemed like too much effort, so we read read instead. Both of us will read almost anything available in English - and the longer the better. Robert struggled through *War and Peace* and I was disappointed that he didn't love it as much as I had.

Robert has been reading Gabriel Garcia Marquez since the DVD supply ran out. He suggests that Marrakesh is like South America - the sense of time is quite different from time in Europe and the US. We have been here for almost six months now, and it seems both like a very short time and a very long time. All we really know is that we don't want to go back to New York in the least.

Robert was quite as productive as in New York - has produced a wonderful full-life sized painting of a donkey that fascinated Mimi when he was working on it - or maybe the warmth of the computer she sat on brought the contented glow to her pregnant face. I write things but I don't bother to send them out. The world isn't exactly waiting with bated breath for my thoughts. It's like being on a permanent vacation - little pressure except from myself to do anything much. A long time ago we toyed with the idea of running a happiness hotel for retired hippies - then decided they wouldn't pay and would squabble and the whole thing would be a disaster.

We think we may be going to break down and buy a proper cooking stove - with four burners and an oven. Oh joy! Then we can dump the Turkish camping gas thing and stop pretending we are camping out and then get the stairs tiled...

We spend most afternoons sitting at Cafe France admiring the various costumes, and looking out for donkey carts and trying to avoid the man with the two stringed banjo who we call Twanger who people give money to to make him go away.

The sun was very hot this afternoon, and walking home about seven the light was casting reflections of palm trees onto a big wall near the Bahia Palace. We arrived home to find Ghislan swabbing down the courtyard having made our bed in a new and different way. Each week we notice small changes in her arrangement of things. She puts the imam's chair near the wall or the cushions in a new design. We look forward to these experiments.

She asked us which of the kittens were boys and which girls and I said I didn't know since I didn't want to upset Mimi and disturb her. Ghislan merely picked them up, inspected them briefly, and put them into two piles - three girls and two boys. In the evenings we watch kitten TV - just observe them tumbling over each other and play fighting and jostling for place at Mimi's nipples. We worry that Blinkie may only have one eye - her fur is so dark and her face is so tiny it's hard to tell. We worry that Baby, the smallest of the kittens, isn't getting enough to eat.

March 2007

Before we came to Marrakesh Robert had been organized and bought tapes and books with Arabic lessons which he had studied both in America and here, and I had tried to learn bits and pieces of Arabic on the street. Altogether we were making some limited progress, but we thought it was about time we learned more. So we went to see the Ismail who works at Sherazade, a most mild and conscientious young man, and asked him if he would come to our house once a week to give us lessons. He said *Inshalla* and arrived at four yesterday afternoon.

We sat at the table in the courtyard and had tea and patisssserie marocaine and learned all the possessives
my pen =stilo de air lee
your pen= stilo de air lik
mother, father, son, daughter
up down, left right and all sorts of other things.

We each wrote it all down phonetically and I felt as if my brain was full to bursting.

We also learned how to say, "No thank you, we don't need your help!" - useful for small boys who pester you and want to show you 'Big Square'.

Pronunciation is critical: what sounds almost the same to us - hkamer - could mean: fill up the gas tank, green, or donkey depending on how you say it.

Our next lesson consisted of learning all the names for various family members and was mind bogglingly complicated. Instead of simply aunt and uncle there are different words for your father's sister and mother's brother and so on and so forth. I fear we will never have use for all the complexities of family relationships.

    Lots to learn.

March 8, 2007

    Bobby arrived from New York via London on Tuesday evening in good spirits. He had brought American Kennel Club UNO - sporting dogs kind, so we played that in the dark on the chilly roof. Bobby only wore a t-shirt having come from England that day. He is camping out on the bed in the salon with Mimi and the kittens.

    That afternoon I had had two sets of people to tea.

    A. told a strange story: she was offered a dog - a female black labrador whose master had been murdered - but thought it might not be a good watch dog. In Morocco one hears all sorts of stories and one never knows which parts of them are true. So much is hearsay and surmise.

    On Bobby's first morning, knowing we had to be home by noon for our Arabic lesson, we walked through Djemma elFna and up to the Mellah market where the younger olive seller was having a violent argument with a fat, older man who looked like a supplier of some sort. Everyone stopped to watch and several men were holding back the main participants to prevent them coming to blows. How much of the threat was bluster and how much real is hard to discern.

    I went back to Aziz, my original flower seller, having tried several others. It's a bit like hairdressers or boyfriends - you are made to feel you are cheating on them, or being disloyal, if you buy from someone else after you have established a relationship. Bobby picked out orange and pink roses.

We arrived home mid-day expecting our second Arabic lesson and waited and waited…then we had lunch. At three I called Ismail.

Conversation as follows:
"How are you, Ismail?"
"Very well, Mrs. Elizabeth, *allhamdullah*. And you?"
"Very well."
"And Mr. Robert?"
"He's very well."
"That's good."
Me: "Ismail, when are we having our next Arabic lesson?"
Ismail : "Tomorrow, *inshallah*."

In the evening we had a turkey and vegetable couscous and I tried to interest Caitlin in adopting a kitten. She sounded more interested in adopting the dead man's dog. Because it was quite windy, we went up to the roof to try to fly Robert's kite but had no real luck. After Caitlin and Samuel had left, we played UNO again - but this time in the courtyard where it was a little warmer and I was able to distinguish between the green and blue cards. I lost.

We wanted Bobby to have an enjoyable and varied visit - not just to hang round with us and the kittens waiting for Arabic lessons.

On Thursday he went with Robert to pick up a Playstation2 for Ismail and in the afternoon we went to Grand Cafe de la Poste for a snack and then to the park with the dinosaurs in.

On Friday I booked to have a driver take us to the Barrage - a vast artificial lake and reservoir formed by damming a river. We got to the lake quickly and without incident - it was large, picturesque and blue and we wandered around it for a while and Robert and Bobby skipped stones.

We then walked back to the car and Mohammed, the driver, said for an extra 50dh gas money we could see lots more things and go on the scenic route back to Marakkesh via Azni. This seemed like a good idea at first. We headed to Amerziz through unpolluted and lovely spring countryside with mimosa and apple and almond blossom; it began to get hilly and we stopped to pick up multi-colored rocks and take a picture of a Berber village which blended into the hillside.

Then the road crossed a little stream and we started climbing upwards and the road became narrower and altogether less road and more track like and the drop to the right more precipitous. The only other traffic we met were 4X4's barreling in the other direction which could cope with the loose piste. Huge boulders seemed likely to tumble from the scrubby vegetation of the mountainside. I'm afraid I was pathetic and anxious and my limited taste for adventure was sorely tested. The mountainous track wound on endlessly.

I was most relieved when we arrived in Azni, having seen lots of mountain goats with kids frolicking beside the road. We stopped for a drink beside the river and a musician played a little impromptu song about Bobby - much more tuneful than usual.

In the evening we went to the Palais Gharnata a restaurant owned by Wafa's family-(she used to work at the American School where her little girl Yasmin is in kindergarten.) Palais Gharnata is near the Bahia palace and is a palace in itself with soaring painted ceilings and a 16th century marble fountain from Italy. In the olden days, marble was traded gram for gram with sugar for marble - the huge Carrara marble pillars in the Medersa benYoussef are other examples.

Our party consisted of Monte, Maryam, Robert, Bobby and me and Wafa and Yasmin. The food - *breewats, tagines* with meat and chicken and fennel and apricots, *pastilla*, dessert *pastilla* and pastries were beautifully served on a rose petalled table.

Yasmin was well behaved and kept wanting to play "Where's Yasmin?" behind my scarf. Wafa said we were in her house and were her guests so we ended up only tipping the waiter and sending chocolates to Wafa later. It's this palace that was the inspiration for Queen Ida's palace in my story *Jane in Winter*.

As well as the Sporting Dogs Uno Bobby bought us a DVD of the complete series of *Twin Peaks* which we watched in the salon as the girls in the other half of 115 giggled. How strange to live in such close proximity with people we have never seen but often hear. Their brother occasionally peers over the roof that separates our terraces but tries his best not to be caught.

We had to do business things in America and were away for two weeks leaving the house and kittens in Ismail's hands. We arrived home to find the five kittens in fine and bouncy fettle and rushing about the place at alarming speed, fighting with each other and climbing up things with insatiable curiosity. As I write, they are taking clipped off palm and papyrus leaves out of a blue plastic bucket in the courtyard.

One evening, when the kittens had been clawing their way up Robert's jeans, he felt fluid running down his leg. He wondered if he was bleeding, but instead discovered clear fluid, not blood. What on earth could it be? In the end we worked out that the kitten's needle claws had pierced the skin - but not deeply enough to draw blood.

The plants were all flourishing - the plumbago and the blue privet type thing in particular.

Ismail was cheerful and it was good to see him. He had fun flying the radio controlled helicopter in the courtyard, and, when he returned to pick up his television set and perfume, dabbed lavish samples of 'Chevrolet' - it comes from Italy- behind our ears - so we smelled like twenty-three year year old Moroccan fashionistas for the rest of the day. Ismail said that the garbage collectors, who I often tipped, asked for money every day before nine and it drove him crazy. He said that the two boy kittens were '*mechan*t'.

The weather was perfect - warm and sunny but not at all hot. When we went on the bus up to Gueliz to re-supply the fridge with beer and potato chips we got a religious bus going with extracts from the Koran blaring from the radio and a 'Dancing with the Stars' blaring Brittney Spears one coming back. The driver is allowed to choose which station is on. Sometimes it's the French equivalent of PBS.

Yussef at the hanut and grandpa at the general store were pleased to see us and said kind things about Robert's attempts at Arabic.

Once we had bought roses and olives at the Mellah market we felt right at home.

April 2007

Mimi has been spending increasing amounts of time outside on the roof or in the alley because she is losing interest in being jumped on and generally annoyed by five wild little creatures with needle teeth and enchanting faces.

We rarely know what she gets up to. The other day, when returning from Gueliz, burdened down with bags of new kitty-litter, Robert ran into Mimi at the top of derb Djedid, eating the food put out on dirty plastic for the other Mimi - the fattest cat in the world. Robert wanted our Mimi to follow him home and she did for a bit and then turned back and went off to steal some more food.

Yesterday she was very proud of herself: she brought home a chicken head for her children to eat. The chicken head has now vanished but we have no idea what happened to the beak.

I have been working at the American School again this week - 4th Grade this time - where, instead of Mrs.Witch, I was called Mrs.Whiz which is more fun. When you get up early you see a different Marrakesh, but since it is spring many more people are about early unlike in the dead of winter where no one is stirring before 9am. On Tuesday afternoon we were told all the roads were closed because the King and his entourage were leaving town and we might be trapped at school for several hours - but luckily the roads had opened again by 3:30.

When the King is in Marrakesh the compound near the American School where his sister lives has groups of three guards posted at short intervals round the walls. The three consist of: one in a khaki normal soldier outfit, one in a dark blue police uniform and the third in a magnificent scarlet tunic who somewhat resembles a hussar - what's a hussar? asked Robert and I said something out of the 19th century.

    The countryside looks fresh and greenish and it's good to be out of the city with the children. From the lunch terrace at the school you can look towards the mountains, and in another direction towards the city where the Koutoubia is mistily visible above the smog. Yesterday afternoon there was a wild wind and black threatening sky and all the glass lanterns in the open hallways swung perilously and the canopies over the picnic tables blew over. The pay for substituting at the American School is almost more trouble to collect than to earn. First you have to make a list of the days when you have worked and then make an appointment with the bursar's secretary. Then you have to petition the bursar himself. The next day you can collect your money.

    The kittens are now two months old and two of them - Bitey and Blinky went to live amongst peacocks, rabbits and a large dog in the country at Maryam and Chris' house. Blinky turns out to have two perfectly good eyes and has been renamed Bisous which means kisses. The children, Skylar and Tristan, seem thrilled with the kittens who replaced a poor young cat who had died.

    Poor Mimi wandered round the house crying and looking for Bitey and Blinky all night but now has settled down to enjoy Booger Junior - who now hangs out under the kitchen counter on a pink floor cloth with a gray vase - and Ollie and Baby. They are all now fat and very energetic.

    At book club we discussed *The Year of the Elephant* a Moroccan novella dealing with the period of resistance to the French. The main character smuggles arms and sets fire to shops. Is she a freedom fighter or a terrorist? As usual, we came to the conclusion that it depends which side you are on - one side always wants to demonize the other. Then a discussion of whether we were getting terrorism updates here - after the suicide bombings in Casablanca. My take is that there really isn't too much you can do about anything like that - the IRA in London in the 70's, the Twin Towers - Virginia Tech. You could live your life in constant fear or just try to get on with it. A friend's mother died in the Egypt Air crash in 1998 - that a case of 'workplace rage' rather than terrorism. She's still dead.

    I spent yesterday taking all the pieces of glass out from the insets above the interior doors - it was a not-very-pretty yellow with a pattern in it - like a bad 1950's bathroom. I went up to the Place des Ferblantiers (tinsmiths' square) where the glass cutters work. This is a perilous occupation and many of the workers are missing parts of their hands. I had them cut glass for our bathroom window glass in bright clear colors - the only problem is that it lets in less light - but now there is brilliant blue, red and green glass that casts reflections on the polished plaster. The glass is fixed in with little tacks, not putty, and I managed the whole thing by myself.

    Hotel Tazi has the only bar in the Medina that serves alcohol which makes it a magnet for every ne'er'do well in town.
    Perhaps, once it was lovely - all that decorated plaster work, pink-veined marble on the walls, marble stairs, pierced brass lanterns, painted woodwork and so forth - but thirty or more years of cigarette smoke and abuse have rendered it tawdry and tired. The oversized arm chairs and sofas in the lobby, slip-covered in red and yellow flocked velvet, have high tide marks on the backs - what possible flood could have entered Tazi? Maybe Moroccan maids sluicing vainly from enthusiastic buckets.

After a shwerma for lunch, Robert wants a beer and we find a battered sofa at Tazi and admire the other, mostly ancient clientele. The desk clerk looks like PeeWee Herman - sounds like PeeWee Herman; his face is quite white. The cheerful waiters have food stains on their uniforms. Ours tells us mint tea is Moroccan whiskey - a very old joke like a donkey being a Moroccan Mercedes. The door man has a metal scanning wand but doesn't use it - if it even works at all.

A French couple, bright scarlet on one side, lard white on the other, from some expedition to the mountains, order both beer and wine. Then come the parade of fabulous elderly men with henna-ed hair and grease shined suits, and then one, chomping on a cigar, who looks like King Farook: striped shirt belted into white, tight pants -waist size approaching sixty inches at least. I wonder how many designs there are in the room as the King stares at us from his wedding picture in front of the digital clock. It doesn't in the least matter what time it is.

When we were first in Morocco while waiting to get into our house that burning hot September, I went in search of Tazi's swimming pool and walked down an endless corridor off which sprang countless little rooms, each one the setting for some horrible demise. Tazi pool is one of the very few on the planet which didn't tempt me. It was a gleaming chartreuse green.

In Tazi's bar people watch soccer on a large TV which is reflected in the glass doors. Robert says Fellini used to hang out in a seedy hotel in Rome full of White Russians looking for Gothic characters. Tazi is a little like that.

A low end excursion group appears, rumpled and surprised to have returned alive from wherever they went. They order more beer.

While walking back from Hotel Tazi, I noticed a large group of small boys giggling outside Riad Isis. Drawing closer, I discovered the cause of their merriment. A large uncouth creature was mounting a poor little cat…Mimi needless to say.

So I stamped my foot and both animals fled. Stupidly, I said to the small boys that I wanted them to catch Mimi and bring her home. The only reason I wanted her was that her appointment at the vet was on Tuesday.

So every small boy in derb Djedid - probably about twenty of them - set off in hot pursuit of her.

"*Vous me donnez un piece?*"

"Only if you find her and bring her to my house."

Trying to describe her, all I could come up with was that she had '*beaucoup de colours*'.

Chaos ensued.

Hammering on the front door. Small boys with a large orange male cat.

No, a small cat. Female.

Hammering on the door. Small boys with a small orange cat. No.

"*Vous me donnez un piece?*"

No.

Hammering on the door.

Robert says don't ever, *ever*, ask small boys to do anything, ever again.

"We've found her in a house," a small boy says.

"Then bring her here."

Hammering on the door. No Mimi. "She scratched me. Give me a little coin."

Meanwhile Robert was on the roof trying out the new barbeque. In all the confusion I had put the black bag of charcoal out in the garbage pile in the derb and had to get new charcoal.

Much more hammering on the door and tweeting of the doorbell and eight small boys, all with their hands outstretched, bring Mimi home. I grab her and try to close the door which is pushed open again as a great sea of boys plunge headlong into the hall.

Amidst all the clamor, I give the largest boy 10 dihram - about $1.25 - the agreed price for finding the damn noisy cat - and all the others say they want money too.

Each individual suggests that it is he who personally did something or other.

The knocks on the door and the tweeting of the doorbell last for about another hour until Robert goes out looking fierce and tells them *baraka* in no uncertain terms.

The cat is back. She continues yowling quite unfazed by all this excitement.

Then one last, sad little boy stands at the door and tearfully explains that it really was him who found Mimi. I believe him and give him five dihram.

Yesterday Ghislan took Booger Junior to live with Loobna. She said he was more *zween* (handsome) than Ollie and stuffed him into her handbag and set off down the derb. Now we are down to two kittens. Ollie is getting fatter.

Mimi is off to the veterinarian in Gueliz to be spayed since we do not need an endless supply of kittens. She is zipped into a rush basket for the trip.

Yesterday the electricity was turned off from 9am until 5pm. in order to upgrade the service from 110 to 220 volts. This was a great hardship since we are both addicted to the internet - I think we would bore each other to death without it. It was also an overcast, dull day and hard for Robert to paint.

It made me feel even more sorry for the people in Baghdad who, as well as being in the middle of a historic disaster, only get three to six hours of electricity a day.

Then I went up to the vet - tripping headlong on uneven paving stones on the way. I picked up a very groggy, and mercifully doped up and now silent Mimi. The poor veterinarian's arms were covered in silver ointment where Mimi had scratched her horribly badly. While waiting for a taxi to go home, I saw a man walking along Mohammed V with a bedraggled looking peacock under his arm.

The kittens did not recognize their three-days-absent mother with a great bandage round her middle and hissed at her.

In the late afternoon, when the lights finally came back on, we discovered, to our delight that they are - miraculously - about 30% brighter and we can actually see in the kitchen.

After cooking burgers on the new barbeque on the roof, we set off in search of ice-cream in Djemma elFna and had rarely seen the square so packed with a milling mass of people. A whole group of young Moroccans were wearing yellow green and red wooly hats with faux dreadlocks hanging out of them. A baby in a stroller was wearing his best outfit - a snow suit. The fishing poles were set out to fish for soda and the blind violinist was extra tuneful. The Kotubia loomed above the tall stand of trees and it was altogether most picturesque.

Derb dabachi, on a Saturday night was packed with the usual raucous vendors hawking awful cheap 'designer' clothing. There was such a crush it was almost impossible to make our way down the street but everyone was in a holiday mood.

I suddenly thought: I have not the least idea what's going on, I don't know what the relationships are between men and women, what people think about religion, education and progress, the environment - anything. I felt both comfortable and utterly foreign.

As an ex-pat one soon discovers others in the same boat. I had been to a planning meeting for a proposed American Women's Club of Marrakesh held at the Hotel Toulousian. Judy is rather keen on it and we hope to provide a guide for newcomers to Marrakesh with lists of doctors and dentists and clubs and all those things most of us had to fumble towards. I proposed a video and book swap. I thought we should have 'English-Speaking' rather than American in the name of the club because I'm not very pleased with being American right now. There are a number of British women who would be potential members. Would English-speaking Moroccan women be allowed to join? Of course.

In response to this women's group, Robert proposed The Interplanetary English Speaking Men's Club: Marrakesh Chapter. The first meeting was to be held in the lobby of Hotel Tazi where the members would drink beer and not do anything useful.

So Robert went off to meet with other interplanetary types while I stayed at home in peace. After a couple of hours I decided to see what was going on, but when I turned to lock the front door I discovered that something - possibly a matchstick - had been jammed into the lock so it was impossible either to lock the door or open it. I was shut out with no way to get in since the house has no windows and only the one door. The cats were imprisoned.

I rushed off and retrieved Robert from Tazi. He was furious of course. And of course it was Sunday afternoon when no one was around. I couldn't phone Ismail since I was locked out from my landline. I asked at the *hanut* and was taken to Ismail's house where I met his mother for the first time. Like Ismail, she was slim and elegant. She provided his phone number and I went to Riad Cristina to borrow a phone to call him.

In the interim several small boys and Mustafa the cigarette seller all tried to help Robert get the wood out of the lock with, variously, a spanner, a paper clip and another key. No dice. Half an hour later Ismail arrived on a bicycle and eventually helped Robert break into the house by shifting the whole door sideways.

How much trouble a little sliver of wood can be! Who on earth has time to do anything as silly as putting something into a lock? Hm...well, one of the army of small boys who haunt the derb with not much to do at all and lots of time on their hands. Robert suspects a fat, smirky little boy he doesn't like at all who had asked Robert for money during the searching for Mimi debacle.

On Monday I took Mimi to have her bandage changed. She again travelled on the bus zipped into the wicker basket. She emerged from the vet - having scratched the poor woman very deeply again - with a very un-chic plastic halo collar and a tummy painted silver. Had the other cats in the derb had the chance to see her, they would have laughed themselves silly. Now there is silver ointment smeared over everything. While waiting to get a taxi back from the vet, I saw a white horse, entirely alone, walking round the roundabout and then heading down Boulevard Mohammed V. No one took any notice of it at all.

May 2007

Another wine tasting, this time hosted by Susan at her office in Gueliz where two conference tables were pushed together and many glasses set up amidst roses and candles. The usual gang attended including Andrina, the Scottish physical education teacher from the American School whose glitzy, spangled attire and glamorous make-up makes me feel frumpy and Moroccans wonder about her morals. She says when she goes out to nightclubs the local good time girls fear she is competition and are rude to her.

The theme of the wine-tasting was Spanish and South American red wine served initially with the labels covered up. The first wine was a pretty, clear ruby color and went down smoothly, the second had a slightly rusty brownish tinge and tasted metallic. Numbers three and four were the South American, but by that time they just tasted the same to me.

At first we pretty much stuck to discussing the wine, then later on full of booze and snacks, the conversation turned to how everything is changing so quickly - how once it was possible to look down Boulevard Mohammed V to the Kotubia and not see a single car, and how pretty Gueliz was when there were only little villas with gardens and no high rise buildings at all. Who is to live in all these new buildings? The general consensus is that they were built as investments and possibly to launder drug money after France adopted the Euro. Who knows? Possibly just another of the many Marrakshi stories whose veracity is impossible to ascertain - like the story that Chelsea Clinton owns a cavern under the big hill behind Marjane.

Another brief anecdote. Craig's kitchen looks out onto the roof of a mosque where people throw garbage. He asked the mezzuin if he could pay to have the debris removed. The mezzuin gladly agreed. Shortly thereafter the roof was covered in garbage again - including liquor bottles.

It grew quite dark and the candlelight threw the reflections of the bottles against the wall. When it came time to vote on the wines - Mary M is most particular about recording such things - we decided that the first one, a Spanish rojha was the best - the last two had sort of cruised by in a blur. Andrina emptied all the dregs from all the glasses into her glass and swigged the contents.

May 5th

On Fridays widows sit outside the doors to the mosques waiting to receive charity. They arrive very early in the morning and sit, in pitiful heaps of drab clothing, all day mutely imploring passersby to give them something, however small. Very recent widows are dressed all in white from head to toe - a sort of reversal of being a bride. I carry small change with me and hand it out to as many women as I can.

There are huge numbers of mosques, several with walking distance of everyone. Only men attend the mosques since women are considered to be holy enough already and can say their prayers at home.

The other day when I went to buy onions from the man under the banyan tree on rue riad zitoune la'kadim, I ended up waiting for what seemed a hugely long time. It would have been rude just to go home sans onions because no one should lose business because he is saying his prayers.

There are beggars everywhere and large numbers of people whose disabilities are so horrific it is hard to look at them. One man's leg was such a mass of open sores I merely thrust money into his hand and rushed off. One of the saddest beggars sits in his wheelchair outside the patisserie on Princes in the evenings. His body is twisted and wasted in the last stages of some awful degenerative disease. What is worse is that his eight or nine year old daughter is made to stand beside him gazing up at you with tears staining her grubby cheeks at a time when she should be in bed. This works terrifically well as a begging strategy, but breaks my heart nonetheless.

The other day I saw an earnest young woman, possibly a college student, kneeling down with a clip board next to a beggar woman on derb Dabachi and asking her questions for some sort of survey. I wonder what the questions were?

Hard to justify one's responses to so many in real need. I give money whenever I can, which is pretty often, and see it as a sort of small daily tax on being a fortunate person in a world where so many are not fortunate.

Because the light here is so bright, the reflections so amazing, and everything crying out to have pictures taken of it, I decided to take up photography. Claudia is a wonderful photographer. I study her work - her close attention to light and shade and shadows in particular.

My first camera was a Kodak Brownie, in the days you had to wait for a week to get your photos back from Boots and then half of them were awful, not to mention you had to pay for them. Now things are digital you can take as many pictures as you want and discard all the hopeless ones. In London I had a black and white Poloroid camera but my photos were so dull, and the film so expensive, I abandoned it. I was very slow to understand digital cameras, but, since this morning, I have become a shutter bug.

It was incredibly hot last week. The sort of weather where you plan your day round what you think you can bear and hide mid-day. Getting out of the city was an excellent idea. So on Sunday we went to the Barrage where we had been with Bobby in the early spring. There we drank wine – Moroccan and Italian – and ate salad, brochettes, and fruit on a terrace overlooking the lake with the Atlas Mountains in the distance.

The landscape reminded me of the backgrounds in Piero della Francesca's paintings – rather arid and with little round hills and well defined trees.

After lunch David Hales and I swam in the lake and it was wonderfully refreshing - ie rather cold. There were lots of families there – and lots of people splashing about in the water.

May 24th

The weather, having cooled off after we went to the Barrage, has warmed up again. 101F yesterday. Lovely and cool in the morning but you know it is just going to get hotter and hotter.

I'm doing odd days here and there at the The American School which has huge windows and a breeze blows through the whole building but by 3:30 in the afternoon, while waiting outside to go home, the sun is a torment – and even worse is walking across Djemma elFna in the late afternoon.

On Monday we told Ghislan not to sweep the roof as it was just too brutal up there and retreated to Cafe France where we watched the world go by – and some of the world was still wearing its winter overcoat. A caleche driver was wearing two jackets – the tourists next to nothing which is sometimes regrettable.

Baby, the littlest kitten, having been let outside the front door to taste the delights of life in the derb, has vanished. After my initial panic, and realizing that I would be thought quite mad if I knocked on every door in the derb asking for her, I resigned myself to her loss. Since Mimi arrived unannounced at our house as a healthy young kitten – all clean and well fed – we are hoping Baby has followed her mother's example. Since we haven't heard her crying – or seen anything worse – we are assuming she has taken up with some other family.

Neither Mimi nor Ollie seem to have noticed her absence. I bought them flea repellant at a pharmacy near Marjane this morning – having remembered that fleas were *puce*.

At a birthday party last Saturday night we met a whole cross section of expatriates and had all sorts of polglot conversations over the loud beatings of drums which formed the entertainment. I have never quite understood the attractions of gnawa music. A German said he was a great friend of the owners of swanky Riad Noga and assured me that his friend's best guests were always the English. I'm not quite convinced that this is always the case.

Everyone here seems to have some sort of business venture – tourism or making caftans or designer clothing, jewelry or tiles. I toyed with the idea of opening an English tea shop – scones and clotted cream etc but am much too lazy, in spite of the many potential customers.

We bought two CD's last night in the souks – were assured that both were in English. One was: a perfectly awful film with Sean Penn pretending to be a Pulitzer Prize winning poet. Tonight's attempt at watching The Wind That Shakes the Barley was the usual disaster - all sorts of audio suggestions and subtitles but only actually playing in French. We abandoned the effort. Some of the pirated movies show people in the movie theater where the film was illicitly recorded wandering across the picture on their way to the bathroom.

June/July

When it is incredibly hot roses' heads droop in about twenty four hours – unlike in the winter when they can last two weeks. So now we have lilies instead.

All houses have their little quirks:

In ours you have to sneak up on the kitchen tap and turn it off REALLY FAST or it won't turn off at all. Sometimes the metal handle falls off into the dishwashing water because it isn't attached very well.

You have to hold the gas on for at least twenty seconds for it to remain lit.

You have to pull the front door towards you and slightly upwards while you lock the top…and so on.

The other day, on the way back from Marjane, loaded down with groceries, I waved in the general direction of the cart men as I got out of the taxi by Cafe France. Two men with carts approached me and each indicated that I had summoned him. The taxi driver helped me get all the stuff out of the back of the taxi. Which cart man to take?

They were very angry with each other.

Which of you was first?

Both insisted it was him.

I looked at the taxi driver who shook his head. This all went on for a very long time. In fact I wasn't sure when it would end. Both cart men were in their fifties.

Finally, I gave one man 10dh and told him to go away and had the other man put my groceries in his cart and off we went down Dabachi. I paid the second cart man 20dh. Sad when World War III is about to break out over so little money.

Mr. Booger, a rather battered cat of unattractive appearance but appealing character is trying to worm his way into our affections by trying to clean up his act. He hangs out on the roof a lot and likes to be petted – when one can bear to do so. He also likes food. We gave him a Frontline flea treatment which I hope he is grateful for. Needless to say, we quite like him…merely on the strength of the fact that he seems to like us. He is always trying to break into the house and when he does he squirts urine onto the stairs before I hustle him out of the front door. Shortly thereafter he reappears on the roof.

We have been in America for our son's wedding. A most happy event. When we returned to Marrakesh, we found the house covered in a film of sand and dust. There had been a sandstorm in our absence so Ghislan had not let us down. Robert swilled down the courtyard to get rid of some of the dust and cobwebs and washed what remains of the ivy. It's amazing how quickly grime accumulates here. We also picked dead leaves off all the plants on the terrace.

I walked by Sherazade to see if Ghislan was there since even more scrubbing is in order, only to discover that, according to Loobna, "Ghislan is in another city". I suppose on vacation. According to Mary M people get three weeks vacation so who knows when she will re-appear.

Things that have vanished during our absence are: a little red plastic spray bottle, the good bread knife and a wooden chopping board.

Having quite given up on Mimi since we had not seen her for four days, Robert discovered her on the roof with Booger this morning. She looks well, plump and fluffy, so perhaps all the time she has another family somewhere. Ollie was pleased to see her and licked her and then started fighting with her so she has gone back on the roof. I realize that I must really not get too attached to Moroccan ally cats since they come and go entirely as it pleases them.

August in Marrakesh is intolerably hot and anyone who can possibly escape does so. We were happy when our friends Maryam and Chris asked us if we wanted to share the beach shack they had rented for the month outside Essouira. This sounded wonderful since they were only going to be there part of the time and we could borrow their very beat up Renault Diesel. They explained that the house wasn't on the beach but quite near it.

We left Marrakech about nine in the morning leaving the grittiness and fumes of the town behind, getting stuck behind vast lorries belching other fumes with their loads threatening to overturn, and various hay carts similarly overburdened. We were overtaken by speeding clapped-out Mercedes grand taxis. We passed through Chichaoua then crossed the bleak almost lunar landscape with outcroppings of rock where the land seems vast until we reached the verdant agricultural uplands with olives and Argan trees which surround Essouira. We arrived at Kilo 8, a restaurant eight kilometers outside town, in the middle of the day as the wind was blowing so much sand in the air everything looked brownish-gray. It was at least fifteen degrees cooler than in Marrakesh. Here we turned off the road onto unpaved rocky piste in search of 'the beach shack'. We found the double garage doors Maryam had described with little difficulty and found the door into the garden. The only problem was they key would not open the door.

After numerous efforts to get in, we realized it was

probably bolted from inside. I finally accosted a young man who went into the adjoining house and we managed to gain entry. The 'beach shack' turned out to be a spacious 1950's villa with astoundingly awful decor and furnishings. There was enough seating for about thirty people all covered in bright blue fabric with sparkles in the two salons but the beds were very small – made for midgets and covered with leopard and zebra pattern acrylic blankets. The big bathroom sink merely trickled brackish brown water.

In the dimly lit kitchen a gas stove had six possible burners two of which actually worked - but only if you lit the middle one first. The TV showed CNN and about eight channels in German. The chandeliers shone gold against a PeptoBismol pink ceiling.

Robert did not notice how low the bathroom lintel was until he almost knocked himself unconscious. The villa adjoined the cemetery of the little hamlet. We made contact with Zaineb the maid who Maryam had hired for the month. We didn't think we needed but a maid but since Zaineb needed the work, as so many Moroccans do, we arranged for her to do our breakfast and make us dinner that night.

Zaineb was an excellent cook and made us chicken and fried potatoes which she served to us in the salon. I said she could go home to her family and clear up in the morning, but she preferred to wait in the kitchen as we ate - standing in the dark just waiting. I found this rather unnerving and sad.

When you climbed on to to the roof of the beach shack at night you could see every star in the universe and the pale swath of the Milky Way – at least we think it was the Milky Way.

As you drive into Essouira you pass lots of young men dangling keys who draw a little sketch of a house in the air then tilt their heads on their hands and pretend to go to sleep. They are advertising rooms to rent to people who arrive without bookings. It is an easily understood pantomime.

Unlike Marrakech which is all pink and red, Essouira is blue and white – quite a refreshing change. And there was the Atlantic of course, chilly to swim in, with the lovely refreshing breeze, but the water so cold you need a wetsuit to really enjoy going in. At Sidi Kauoki camels wandered on the beach and vanished into the mist. When you had walked for a long time and vanished into the mist too and thought you were quite alone you would suddenly be approached by vendors selling Rolex watches.

At Moulay Bouzektoun, a tiny village some twenty five kilometers north of Essouira, a mosque sits high on a cliff above the rocky beach almost threatening to tumble onto the sands. There we found designs on the beach made by sand snails -some of the trails go in almost straight lines and others merely go round in circles as if drunk. There were lots of pretty sea urchin shells in varying shades of green and gray.

One day when Maryam and Chris and their children and their maid were with us at Moulay Boukerktoun we threw huge sticks into the crashing Atlantic surf for Rocky their inexhaustible dog to retrieve. This game delighted Rocky and made Robert's arm quite sore with the effort.

Maryam and the children collected piles of interesting rocks to put in the garden of the home they were building. At the end of the day, everything was loaded into the SUV - five adults, two children, the chairs and the picnic things, the towels and the interesting objects collection. It was not until we were back in Essouira buying snacks that we realized that Rocky was missing. A panic. What if Rocky had decided to follow the car down the road and had been killed by a truck? We rushed back expecting at every moment to find his carcass beside the road. We parked by the little cafe where we had stopped before - and there - *alhamdulillah* - was Rocky waiting patiently for us. We gave him a whole bottle of mineral water as his prize for being abandoned for two hours. He gulped this down with glee.

Maryam and I spent time writing our blogs in the little cafe by Kilometer 8 where there is internet access. Hers was rather glamorous and exciting and mine much more mundane. The butcher's stand beneath the cafe was surrounded by the usual attentive audience of cats and dogs. In the evenings we sat in the pink salon of the beach shack flipping channels on the TV to see what strange programs might be beamed to us from the who knows where. The bathroom taps grudgingly dripped brown water.

Back to School September 8th 2007

I have agreed to do another stint of teaching at the American School teaching the four year olds. As usual I have to get up early to catch the bus in Gueliz with the other teachers, teachers assistants, maids and groundskeepers. The school provides a real American School bus – a Bluebird of antique vintage. In America school buses are always yellow. In Marrakesh the bus is white. I'm not quite sure where the bus started life but it spent time in both in Tangier and Rabat before ending up here. This morning it started its journey in Gueliz, headed out past Bab Khemis and Metro and then, after grinding miserably for a few minutes, died beside the road some five kilometers short of the school.

Everyone laughed.

Almost the entire staff of the school was on the bus…there would be no one to open the gate even.

The acting headmistress of the lower school and the man who opens the gates were the first to stand beside the road to flag down passing parents. Pretty soon we had all hitched rides and school began as usual.

We are not sure what the prognosis for the bus is. Its companion bus – the one that used to sit in the school parking lot to be cannibalized for parts – vanished over the summer.

In the classroom I discover that Danah has wonderful shoes with pink hearts and glitter to start the school year.

Inspired by Danah's shoes, I decided it would be nice for the children to make a greeting card with a heart on the front to color and give to someone in their family. Since they can't write yet and some speak little English, I said I would write the name of whoever they wanted to give the card to.

Me: "Who would you like to give your card to?"
Child: "Mama"
Me: "Shall I write 'To Mama' on the front?"
Child, confused, "*One* Mama"

So I did not offer to write For/four Daddy. I'm amazed at how many unseen pitfalls the English language presents.

It is now our second Ramadan in Morocco. As a nominal Christian, I'm allowed to have lunch though I try to be pretty discreet about it when many of the other teachers are observing the fast. They merely recline on the banquettes which line the room and relax while we guilty ones eat.

One day a Muslim friend joined me at the lunch table and opened her Tupperware container of salad. I asked why she was eating and she said she had her period and was therefore unclean. She would have to make up the days at the end of Ramadan. I asked what would happen if she somehow forgot to do so. She looked rather shocked at this suggestion. I heard that one of the mothers of children in the school was determined to fast despite being diabetic. She was eventually persuaded to eat normally since it would be a greater sin to deprive her children of a mother. Pharmacies have posters explaining what medications you can take during the holy month. Young children are allowed to eat normally during the day but are allowed to stay up late with their families which makes for a rather sluggish start to the day since most of them are over tired. Some of the children lie down on the classroom floor whenever they get the chance.

In the late afternoon, when it is very hot, many of the shop keepers in the medina recline on mattresses in the middle of their shops. Few people can really be bothered to sell you things – there is a sort of general parched lethargy. Some people's faces seem to sink into an almost skeletal thinness.

Yesterday afternoon I had agreed to go out looking for fabric up by the Mellah. In one shop I looked upwards through the roof to see a room full of artificial flowers and a portrait of Hassan II looking down at me. I don't think it had been touched for forty years. But on the whole I prefer not to go out in the late afternoons.

At about 6:45 the streets are utterly silenced by the call from the mosque when everyone settles down to their *fitur*.

No mopeds, no children shouting. A moment of bliss.

Robert bought a wooden suitcase on derb Dabachi just outside the woodshop. It has just about everything Morocco is famous for – it's wonderfully attractive and unusual, a real visual delight. Its first drawback as a suitcase is that, empty, it weights at least twenty-five pounds. The second is that it is impossible to open without a wrench.

Robert says it still looks cool and its ancient and grizzled salesman would not let it go for under $12. It is lined with wallpaper with scenic backdrops and holiday gift wrap. We will probably use it to store art materials.

By mid-September we had been in the little house here for more than a year and it was time to do more repairs and updates. Ever since we were in the house the tiny bathroom by the front door and under the stairs had been something of a disaster - with plaster flaking from the ceiling and an ominous bulge just above the toilet itself. The wooden beam had been eaten to bits by termites and was about to collapse. We had the beam removed and now in order to get downstairs we had to navigate a gaping hole in the stairs. This was interesting - particularly when carrying hot cups of tea.

We are having new and wonderful floor tiles installed in the salon and my study downstairs. They were made by our friend Samuel who has set up a factory where the traditional method of tile making is used for creating contemporary designs. They are elegant gray and white swirls. Robert worked with the tile layers and learned the Arabic words for left and right and so forth. We traded one of Robert's paintings for the tiles - a most satisfactory arrangement. We also decided to have the bathroom ceiling replaced and had the outside wall holes plugged with cement. A five hundred year old house provides endless entertainment.

On Wednesday we had three cats – the prodigal Mimi on an extended return visit, Ordinary Ollie her son, and Booger Senior who lives on the roof.

When all the workmen and tiles and cement arrived all three vanished.

Mimi returned, fat and cheerful, later in the day. Booger and Ollie disappeared for two days but have finally decided that the lure of food outweighs any distaste they might have for disturbances to their routine.

After flickering for four days, cutting out, getting bright again, diminishing to almost nothing, about seven one morning the electricity finally went out. We did not know whether this was just our house, the whole street or the entire medina. We had almost begun to believe in djinns.

So we went off for a walk to the Mellah to buy olives in horrible tempers. When we got back, having discovered that the electricity was only off in our house, we summoned Ismail who arrived with his brother and a metal ladder. He summoned an equally tall and thin electrician who discovered that exactly the same problem had occurred as did last year – the rotten wiring had finally burned itself through.

The problem was fixed in about an hour. So much for djinns.

While all this was going on, I took photos of the fruit and flowers on the dining table which formed an inadvertent still life.

The cold water tap in the kitchen now turns off without us having to sneak up on it, and the lavatory in our bathroom no longer runs randomly. Smells come and go – again apparently at random – but that might well be the weather and the drains and who knows what.

One morning I came downstairs to discover a huge scorpion in the courtyard. It was indisputably dead which was something of a relief. I assumed the cats had killed it though neither Mimi nor Ollie were around to show off their prowess. I threw the carcass out into the derb then telephoned all my various friends to ask their opinions. When asked what size and color it was, I said it was sort of brownish black and probably medium sized - it had just seemed huge. My friends then assured me this was the *least* dangerous, or alternately, told it was the *most* dangerous kind.

Annabella suggested that scorpions get stirred up when there is construction or renovation going on in the neighborhood. (The new floor tiles?) Mary M told a chilling story about finding a scorpion climbing up the wall of her infant daughter's nursery. I was told that where there is one scorpion there is certain to be another. Much later on Malin asked me if I was so upset about the scorpions because I suspected witchcraft - a thought that had not occurred to me until then.

Caitlin said they had had their first scorpion sighting that week too and that their brave maid had taken off her plastic shoe and whacked it stone dead. For a few days I was vigilant about looking in my slippers then forgot about it and never saw another one - either dead or alive. I'm told children in the country, for want of anything more exciting to do, poke straws down into scorpion holes to aggravate them so they cling on to the straw and can be captured and played with.

Shortly after the scorpion sighting and the instillation of the new floor tiles, we give a supper party on a damp evening when we decide to eat in my study which doubles as a dining room in inclement weather. I transform my desk into a dining table with bright pieces of cloth bought up by the mellah. My latest piece is bright scarlet sailcloth and rather cheery.

Ismail's mother produces a splendid tagine which is delivered by Ismail's father, a most distinguished looking man who has made the haj. After the food eaten, much wine drunk and the guests had departed, we decided to go to bed and leave the clearing up for the following morning.

In the morning I go down to discover that the tablecloth is now bright blue where it hangs over the sides of the table. The crumpled scarlet napkins are also bright marine blue. I think I have gone quite mad. I shout for Robert to come down to inspect this strange phenomena. I telephone everyone who was at the supper. I do believe we have been visited by djins.

It turns out in the end not to be djins after all, but rather a chemical reaction caused by the damp air interacting with the cement that the tiles were set in and the rather fugitive red dye in the cloth. When I washed the cloth it turned red again.

October 2007

One evening Samuel had a great yearning for Breton crepes so we decided to meet at 7pm in Gueliz where the most wonderful crepes can be had. So we set out at dusk through the almost deserted square past the Kotubia at the witching hour when everything stops for people to break their fast. A very lovely time of day between day and night.

However, when we arrived at the crepe place it was as tightly shut up as we should have known it would be on a Sunday evening in Ramadan. So we set out on a tour of all sorts of other equally deserted places. The pizza parlor: closed. The Chinese food place: closed. The Mexican food place – also closed. Even Catanzaro, the reliable Italian place, was shut. It was almost as if a plague had hit the city.

Eventually, when we were quite starved, and had had a great deal of exercise, we came upon a rather middle of the road hotel with a small swimming pool where we discovered they served Thai food.

What to order? How to order?

"Wahed green curry, s'il vous plait."

We speak varying amounts of French and are having Arabic lessons. English is the default mode. Can one use three languages in one sentence?

The Thai curry was delicious, the spring rolls crunchy and there were lots of desserts. They also served beer.

Caitlin and Samuel also like chwarma and we often meet them for lunch. Chwarma is Moroccan fast food – or as close to fast as it is likely to get. It basically consists of chicken cooked the same way Greek gyros are, turning endlessly on a spit. One would imagine it would kill you in an instant, and for ages we avoided it, but now have decided it is delicious. There are four chwarma joints on rue prince Moulay Rachid, that undistinguished street off Djemma elFna very popular with tourists and beggars and sellers of cheap novelties. The one we like best has three floors and a good view of the action in the street below. To get to the terrace you have to climb two flights of rickety stairs – recently covered in hardboard - and duck your head even if you are a very short person. The tables are small and the whole place is greasy. They serve a drink called "Hawaii" which comes in a can and tastes of all the worst cheap candy of your childhood.

Four cats watch your every move, ready to pounce on any lumps of unidentifiable chwarma you toss in their direction.

Our friend Ira, my boss in a previous life, has arrived to stay. We have installed him in my study where there is a spare bed and a shower and a door that locks. Together we have have been doing all sorts of wandering around looking at places that I've neglected for a long time. How easy it is to start taking for granted things which are quite strange and wonderful.

Less strange and a great deal less wonderful are all the omnipresent mopeds which clutter the lanes and alleys, fill them with nasty, polluting fumes and threaten to knock you down. They make walking in the medina an unpleasant hazard and, I'm quite certain, ensure a significant portion of the visitors never return.

Ira gets the award for our best guest, the one who causes no trouble at all and brings home little pastries almost every day where he returns from his daily run round Cyber park in his shorts. He even takes himself off for an excursion to the desert where he rides on a camel and has a wonderful time and returns with a decorated tent peg. He says he leads quite an exciting life for a neurotic person. In Essouira we eat lots of fish fresh off the dock and wander round the derelict mellah. It is the only place where we feel uncomfortable when a man turns to us hissing something about *Juif* - so we beat a hasty retreat.

While changing planes at Casablanca, Ira had met an American couple also on their way to Marrakesh who own a charming modern apartment in Gueliz where we have dinner. Mary's brother is a diplomat and they mostly spend time in rather more swanky circles than ours. However they accept our invitation to supper. Their driver deposits them at Dour Groua and we lead them through the derb. Ismail's mother makes a splendid tagine and as we eat in the courtyard white petals from the jasmine from the upper landing fall confetti-like on the table. Our visitors are enchanted - not having spent too much time in the depths of the medina.

I take Ira to Maison Tiskwin, Bert Flint's house which contains his personal collection of fabrics, jewelry, carpets, baskets and lots of wooden carvings from all parts of the Sahara where the Touareg and other tribes once wandered. Bert Flint, a Dutchman, is now very old and rather deaf but still presides over forty years of treasures. There are wonderful old maps on the walls and two courtyards – one with blue and white tiles.

In tour guide mode, I also take Ira to the Bahia Palace. Bahia means beautiful and the palace is lovely indeed. You walk through the outer garden replete with cats, kittens and banana trees, pass through two courtyards then a large hall with splendid painted ceilings and painted doors and shutters. It took fourteen years to build starting in the 1860's. In 1908 Pasha Glaoui decided it would be a wonderful venue to entertain French visitors. The French were so impressed that they decided to get rid of Pasha Glaoui and installed the *resident-generaux* there. The furniture has long since vanished.

If you were a woman confined to this splendid palace where the singers were blinded so they could not look upon you, you might have wondered how you could escape through all the pretty, complicated doors and windows. The palace was so huge with so many twisting passages surely there must be some way to get out into the fresh air and bustle of the streets. There were parts of the palace you had never seen – never would see – but also hidden gardens and ceilings decorated with emblems of the world – the sun, the stars, the desert and the sea.

I also take Ira to a dentist in Gueliz to replace a cap which had fallen off one of his teeth. He is rather nervous about the whole thing and we are relieved when we discover that the dentist turns out to be the wife of our notaire.

It was one of the days of Eid el Fitr and a family were off to visit family or friends. I saw them at the bus stop with a little boy of about four being carried on to the bus by his proud father. The boy was wearing a red tarboosh and white robe and was altogether beautifully dressed. I longed to ask if I could take his picture but didn't quite like to. I'm sure his family are incredibly proud of him. I was told that the boy was almost certainly off on his way to the party to celebrate his circumcision. Getting on the bus is always chaotic – a mad rush for the door, flying elbows, fat middle-aged ladies who act as if you aren't there and come at you like violent sofas.

I'm writing this sitting under a tree in Cyber Park, a beautiful vast spreading garden once only walked in by the king. Perhaps a small consolation for not having the internet at home since yesterday afternoon. Cats lounge on the low brick walls and a blue-overalled gardener rakes the gravel with a rhythmic sweep. Birds tweet overhead.

So, one asks oneself – why do you live in a developing country and expect modern conveniences?

After many days of fruitless visits to M. le Directeur of Maroc telecom, the usual thing happened – a young man arrived toward nightfall and restored the internet in less than five minutes. He might have appeared from the ether for all I know. Quite magical.

Our front door was the same sort of depressing brown as almost all of the others on the street. When we painted it black it looked a great deal better. Then I started to wonder if there was some sort of prohibition against black doors and went out looking for ones of other colors. In the end I did find some black ones – but not very many – and felt relieved.

I'm always acutely aware of the possibility of doing the wrong thing and upsetting people. Annabella, who has lived here for years, says she probably upsets people on a daily basis without even realizing it. For example there are so many people I would love to take photographs of like the family with the little boy, but know, in my heart of hearts, that they'd hate it. Who on earth wants to be photographed as a curiosity? I have countless photos of women taken from behind.

Yesterday Robert went to Bab al Chemis to buy hardboard panels to paint on. It is usually difficult to find anyone who knows what a right angle is and who can cut straight.

A sturdy man said of course he knew how to cut panels straight at 90 degree angles —*mashi mushkeel* - no problem. He'd do it immediately.

Robert settled on five dihram for each panel. Mr. Sturdy gave the job to his skinny assistant who was equipped with a handsaw: no t-square and no ruler.

Mr. Sturdy produced a ratty piece of hardboard, and after borrowing a tape measure, the assistant started cutting the five pieces by hand.

Robert couldn't watch so went for a little walk and said he'd be back.

On his return, the thin guy had four pieces cut out of the original hardboard – and was cutting the fifth out of a totally dissimilar material.

Robert said he couldn't use that panel since it didn't match the others. After a brief argument the skinny kid realized that the piece did not match and agreed not to include it. Robert decided to take the original four. But, on inspection, he discovered one of the boards had a nail hole right in the middle of it.

"I can't use this," Robert said.

"You could fill the hole – no problem – *mashi mushkeel*," said the assistant.

"*Kabir mushkeel* – big problem. I wanted one without a hole in it," said Robert.

This reasoning seemed like a mystery to both the owner and his assistant. After ten minutes of shouting and waving of arms and drawing a small crowd, it was agreed that the board did, indeed, have a hole in it and that Robert hadn't ordered a board with a hole in it.

The owner reluctantly accepted that Robert would take three of the five boards originally ordered.

He handed the owner twenty dihrams expecting five dihrams change.

The owner then said he had no change.

Robert said he would wait.

The owner disappeared for two minutes and reappeared with a five dihram coin. He gave Robert his most pitiful, sorrowful, desperate look – hoping for a tip.

Robert took the coin and flipped it to the skinny kid who actually did the sawing. After much handshaking and many pats on the back, they all parted friends.

On the way home Robert passed a small lumber yard with new wood, a T-square and an electric saw.

November 20, 2007

In the early mornings the light falls in a much more interesting way than it does at noon. Because it is November, people are bundled up in all sorts of winter clothes though it gets very warm in the afternoons so one forgets to put on a jacket forgetting that the next morning will be chilly again.

The very small vegetable shop has reopened on derb Djedid – it was there last year for three months and then shut. Now I can get mandarins – which have just come in season – and potatoes without having to cart them for miles and miles.

Robert went to the new town to buy beer and an ink cartridge. I went to the mellah market to buy olives and roses. Pretty sunny flip-flop weather still.

The old cat Mr. Booger has reappeared on the roof. The

plants are still alive and Ollie woke us in the night playing soccer with his pomegranate. Mr. Booger occasionally deigns to play with him.

The other night there was torrential rain and we wondered what would happen if the whole courtyard filled up with water. The cats were terrified by the thunder and lightning. However, the farmers need the water desperately since there has been an awful drought. The water level at the Barrage is meant to be astonishingly low.

The artist Motese has a small shop right next to the cat food shop by the Mellah Market. We have been quite friendly with him for a while – he and Robert chat in a mixture of Arabic and English. Today he was studying a catalogue of paintings by Majorelle -of Majorelle Gardens fame - who worked here in the twenties. He was using this to get ideas for new work. He does a lot of rather contemporary repetitive designs – a nice change from charging Berbers. I have a collection of some fifteen small paintings by him.

When we sit at the table in the courtyard jasmine flowers fall on our heads like confetti as they did at our last supper party. They smell wonderful. The pot is just outside our bedroom door.

November 30, 2007

Everything here is so saturated with color that it dazzles the eyes. In Gueliz most of the buildings have metal grills for security but they are a sort of decorative element too. I was hanging round waiting for the school bus very early in the morning after buying small pastries at the only shop open.

I buy quite a lot of little cakes or oranges or cookies because if anyone is around when you're eating it is polite to offer whatever you have to others. Therefore you are often offered nice food but if you have something you desperately want to eat yourself you have to hide it until you are alone.

November 27, 2007

A large man in a red tarbush was in charge of the mint tea at a storytelling afternoon at a riad near my house. He sat before a big silver tea urn and other, younger men handed round mint tea and delicious little pastries whilst we sat on little chairs in the courtyard under two big orange trees laden with fruit. Because it was late on a November afternoon it was quite chilly and I was glad I had a shawl with me.

The main storyteller was tall, lean and weather-beaten and wore glasses. He was utterly compelling and told a traditional tale in Arabic about a king who lusted after all the young women he met- and how one woman outwitted him. A young woman translated for him after each phrase.

Then a young Welshman told another traditional tale in which an old couple acted as hosts to Zeus and Poseidon when the gods had been refused shelter by other people who, of course, got their come-uppance.

As we walked home the derb was lined with blue-turbaned men holding lighted torches.

A knock on the door and this time it is the fire chief in full spiffy uniform. He's visiting everyone to distribute calendars. We invite him in. He sits at the table in the courtyard. We offer him a cup of tea which he accepts. I augment this with some nuts and dried fruit. We give a donation to the fire department and wonder how long his visit will last. He says his wife would be delighted to meet me so I make appreciative noises but secretly hope this is merely a polite gesture. What on earth would I have to say to her? Luckily this never comes to pass.

November 25, 2007

Mandarins/tangerines have arrived in heaps on stalls on derb Dabachi and in the mellah. They smell of Christmas. There are plums too which are wonderful stewed with custard – or a sort of vanilla pudding that seems exactly like custard.

There has been more torrential rain – to the delight of the farmers and on derb Dabachi you can see the designs in the paving stones when usually are they were hidden beneath a thick coating of grime. All the Moroccans are thrilled with the rain *"alhamdulilah"*.

December 2007

Ollie is fine and gulping down his expensive Whiskas with his fat mother, but he gave us a pretty good scare on Monday morning.

He usually spends the night on the roof with the bad boys and comes down to sleep all day on our bed.

In the morning he shouts at us from the parapet on the terrace so I have to get up and feed him. This is pretty effective since he has a very insistent voice – inherited from his mother.

So on Monday as I am about to get up out of my nice warm bed, there is the most tremendous, frightening THUD.

We realize that Ollie has fallen off the roof into the courtyard. We reckon this is at least thirty feet.

Horrified, I rush downstairs to look for his remains. I can't find his body or any sign of him but eventually discover him under the bed in my study. I eventually lure him out and fifteen minutes later he eats a little breakfast. He has a small bloody scrape on his chin where he banged it and a chip on his front tooth. No other signs of anything.

He rests all that day and the next in front of the sitting room fire.

Yesterday he wanted to go on the roof again.

When Ghislan came on Monday afternoon I asked her if cats fall off roofs often?

She merely shrugged and said, *"C'est normale."*

Ismail came by to see Ollie yesterday and said it was *"Pas normale"*.

Who knows.

This year Eid el Kabir, the big holiday will fall on December 21st, the Winter Solstice, and we were remarking yesterday that we hadn't yet seen any signs of sheep or rams or hay. This morning, as we walked down derb Dabachi, we saw our first ram slung beneath the rider of a moped. Then I realized what all the large blocks of wood I had seen outside the wood shop were for.

In Marjane, the Moroccan equivilent of Tescos or Walmart, there were all sorts of holiday decorations, and, sitting in a sort of cavern of packets of tea, was a man offering samples. He reminded me of Santa in a way with a very benevolent sort of face. But he decided on a purposeful, serious look for his photo.

The taxi ride on the way home took an awful long time – we went via bab Chemis and the junk market nearby where people were selling all sorts of second hand household items – Frigidaires and mopeds and almost everything you can imagine – kitchen sinks too – all in an effort to raise the cash for a ram. The taxi driver said all the little children would cry if they didn't get one.

We chatted to the cab driver about the holiday. He told us that he was going to buy two rams – one for his father who has gone blind from diabetes. Diabetes and tooth decay, he told us, are two unfortunate results of the Moroccans' love of sugar.

Ahead of us in the crawling traffic was a sleek new Mercedes. Our taxi driver told us that rich people don't bother to buy rams - they merely go on vacation to Agadir and Casablanca.

Near our house the charcoal sellers and the little boys selling hay are all set for the big day. Two children were very proud to be riding in a cart with their splendid looking ram. The father was pushing them with their mother walking behind. They were heading down derb Dabachi past all the scores of little boys selling hay and oats and little bags of salt and the knife grinders, charcoal merchants and skewer sellers.

In the morning I completed a task begun about four or even six months ago – which shows what a glacial pace I have slowed down to. To back up: Justin and Teresa, the Canadians we had met when we first moved to Marrakesh, had emailed me about a big plate that they had bought in Marrakesh and really liked.

It was in Marrakech that they discovered, to their great joy, that Teresa was pregnant. In due course of time they returned to Canada, their child was satisfactorily born, and the plate broke.

The plate reminded them of their travels in exotic places so they e-mailed me to ask if I could look for a replacement.

It was then summer and hot. I said of course I would look - but when it got a little cooler. Then I lost the e-mail with the design of the plate on it.

Another photo was sent.

Another month passed then I bought a new plate, very similar as far as I could ascertain, to the first one.

Yesterday morning I went to the post office bright and early and went into the separate entrance for foreign parcels.

Had I bought bubble wrap? No.

I thought the post office had that?

You can buy it in the souks. I thought I knew where.

Then the man who did the packing said: never mind, he would help me, and unlocked a big cupboard and produced a very large, old and battered cardboard box which he proceeded to cut about with a knife until he had formed a pretty impressive protective covering for the plate.

He spent a long time doing this and it looked quite sturdy. At this point it would have been churlish to go off and buy bubble wrap.

Then he took another – this time new – cardboard box to cover the first one – which it didn't quite fit over. The whole thing was wrapped around mummy-fashion with sticky tape and then more sticky tape until it was most impressive.

I wanted to take a photo of it but wasn't quite sure how that would appear to my several helpers.

How did I want to to go. Priority or ordinary?

What's the difference? One is three weeks the other four.

Since I'm sure my friends have quite despaired of ever getting anything, ever, from Morocco, I took the four week option.

I'm also frightened the plate will break en route.

At lunch time two Christmas cards were delivered (which makes our grand total three). One of them was from our Canadian friends and included a picture of their son. I'm feeling rather guilty.

I often have henna designs painted onto my hands by Amina, who works quite near Cafe France and does wonderful traditional complex patterns – much more interesting than the little flower tattoos they try to fob off on you before you know better. I like the ones with Berber elements and checker-board squares. Henna smells wonderful too when it is drying on your hand. I go up to the roof to cook the henna and then pick it off piece by piece. The designs last about five days then get rather scruffy looking.

The Story of a Parcel Update:

Well, the parcel did get to Canada but the plate broke somewhere en route. Teresa thinks this is a sign she should return to Morocco to replace it personally.

At the beginning of December there was a literary and arts festival where events were held in splendid riads lit with the requisite candles and flaming torches. The most haunting was at The Musee de Marrakesh one chilly night where a chorus of twenty four Sufi singers performed *a cappella* followed by a group of musicians including a woodwind flute. There were six candelabras and the flames flickered in the breeze and threw elaborate fleeting shadows.

I have started making Christmas cards. I originally wanted to make complicated wood block prints but my wood engraving tools vanished so in the end I made four different camel designs gouged out of lino with the awkward too-big tools I bought in the mellah. Since they were all quite different and have multiple errors we have decided that we were aiming for the handcrafted look all along.

Last night, when we were half asleep, evil Mimi knocked a brand-new jar of honey off the shelf in the kitchen. It fell onto a little calligraphy decorated bowl of tea bags and smashed that too. Broken glass and honey are are a great joy to come down to at dawn- especially when you had planned on eating the honey for breakfast.

December 7th

I spent the morning writing in the salon by the gas fire. We had lunch on the roof in the almost-too-warm sun and could see the snow on the mountains in the distance. Such incredible contrasts in just two flights of stairs. I'm reminded of Coleridge's *Kubla Khan* - the sunny pleasure dome with caves of ice.

On Saturday we went to a movie at the Palais de Congress - part of the Marrakesh Film Festival for which I have managed to wangle a press pass on the strength of two articles in English language magazine. A wonderful swanky movie theater/auditorium with lots of security people brandishing cell phones and walkie talkies. Very luxe and glam. We were asked for our autographs by a man who, as Robert suggested, was using the scattershot approach - if he asked everyone for their signature, he would, perhaps, in the end, hit upon someone famous.

So far we have seen a Czech film, an American one, a Moroccan one, a Hungarian one and a depressing one from Russia about police corruption.

While walking home down derb Dabachi, we saw an old woman patiently waiting to sell three pairs of very used shoes.

December 22, 2007

Yesterday was Eid el Kabir – the big holiday when all the rams and 'mouton' were slaughtered in people's homes.

I was asked if we were going to have one and when I shook my head the young man said, "Perhaps next year."

In the morning I took a walk up deserted derb Dabachi where all the shops were shuttered. Some young men had set up a huge barbeque – an old metal bed frame over big planks of old lumber – near the little square.

When I walked back from the Place, the first ram's head sat atop the barbeque with two trotters beside it.

Swaggering young men walked in the derbs in blood-splattered clothes - obviously pretty cheerful at the part they had taken in the ceremony.

Quite soon after this Ismail arrived at our house with three skewers of lamb's liver kebabs with salt and cumin and home made bread. Quite delicious. Robert said he would eat his later. Of course he didn't.

The bonfire in the derb Dabachi was huge and exciting a bit like a Guy Fawkes party. The rams' heads blackened in the flames and the sizzling wool smelled like…sizzling wool. It all looks a little like a scene from a horror movie.

Lots of bits of sheep ended up in plastic bags in the derb outside our front door where they leaked blood which puddled and looked depressing. Claudia and her boy friend were due to arrive that evening so I decided to swill the mess down with soapy water. The sight of madame with her blue plastic bucket and mop afforded much amusement to the various passers by several of whom stopped to enjoy the spectacle. One of them said, "You can't clean up all of Morocco, you know!"

December 26, 2007

The day after Christmas Claudia and Adam and I set off to to Essouira on the Supratours bus. Half way there, in the middle of utterly nowhere, a little car decided to make a left turn onto a dirt road quite unaware that the huge bus was hard on his heels.

I watched all this in slow motion, knowing exactly what was about to happen. The bus braked extremely hard but hit the rear of the car. Luckily none of the five people aboard the very small car was hurt but a very long wait ensued with at least eleven men inspecting the bashed-in rear of the car. Finally the police arrived from Chichauoia armed with tape measures. Small boys arrived from out of the ether on bicycles. Other cars stopped and disgorged eager onlookers.

Much of writing of notes and taking of statements, hugging, discussing.

An hour passed, and eventually, we were taken to a restaurant some three miles away to wait for another bus since the original bus was not permitted to continue after an accident.

Adam, not wanting to let an opportunity pass, bought a large heavy geode with a purple inside from the gift shop at the rest stop.

December 28, 2007

In Essouria we walked on the Portuguese ramparts and watched the crashing Atlantic waves beat upon the rocks. At the beach intrepid children braved the frigid waves. Riad al Madina, which may or may not have been where Jimmi Hendrix stayed in Essouira in the sixties, had decorated a little tree with tinsel. In the bakeries were cakes somewhat resembling *bruchee a Noel* - sort of Swiss Rolls with vivid pink icing.

I photographed a beautiful hand painted sign for rat poison above a shop that will sell you stuff to kill almost anything that creeps and crawls. A perfect treasure trove of death. What with the number of cats around, I cannot imagine that there is much of a call for their wares – but perhaps there is.

    In all the time I have been in Morocco I have only seen one rat – dead anyway – and possibly two mice – also dead. Hooray for the cats.

2008 Maroc

After the odd melange of end of year and new year festivities, the first order of business is some sort of clean up - and the medina presents all sorts of challenges. We put out our garbage in black plastic bags by our front door very early in the morning and it is picked up by smartly dressed men in blue and yellow uniforms - that is unless the cats have got there first and ripped the bags apart - which is why you can't put the bags out at night. Then the remaining mess is swept up by men with twig brooms who then ring the doorbell expecting a small tip. When Ismail is in charge of the house they don't ring the door bell so often because he gets grumpy with them.

It rained on my birthday and the courtyard was swilling with water which I swept into the drains. Mimi and Ollie had been howling on the roof in the night since they hated getting wet and prefer snuggling in the salon in the warmth of the gas fire.

In the afternoon I went out to take photos of the puddled streets and all the many barbers' shops on rue read Zitoun l'kadim. As Robert has discovered, going to the barber's is something of a social event and what with shampoo, shave and haircut followed by mint tea the whole process takes the best part of an hour.

On Monday I spent the day with Jamila at her small farm some twenty miles outside Marrakesh. It is my idea of an earthly paradise -a charming small house with a walled garden, set in a larger garden amidst arable land with views of the Atlas Mountains just then ruffled with snow after a recent rainfall. The orchard, several gardens, sheep, chickens and goats are tended with the help of an elderly Berber couple. Ah bliss! such quiet - no mopeds and no one selling anything.

Jamila, who grew up in California, is a painter and has a studio upstairs. She has lived in Morocco for more than thirty years and is married to a Sufi scholar. The house is littered with the toys of her grandchildren who were not there that day. We ate lunch on the upstairs verandah. *R'fissa* or *trid* is chicken and vegetables sopped up with little pieces of torn up pancake. A traditional treat cooked by the wife of the gardener. We ate without utensils in the traditional way straight from the big dish. A large plate of mandarins with leaves still attached was part still-life and part dessert. Jamila told me a little about her life and what Morocco was like so many years ago. The surroundings of the farm reminded me of the Tuscan countryside - all olive groves and lush grass. I can scarcely imagine living anywhere more lovely - or more crying out to be painted and loved.

Animals are so much more part of everyday life in Morocco - the omnipresent cats and the donkeys in the derbs and the horses drawing the caleches. Mimi has become rather stout lately - all that lounging by the gas fire and all that expensive Whiskas from the supermarket. She still eyes the birds on the roof but hasn't eaten one lately - at least so far as we know.

Since life in Marrakesh is becoming familiar and less astonishing, I rarely have the desire to buy anything though I eye old metal bowls and Berber jewelry. I'm still bewitched by the kaleidoscope of colors in the dyers' souk where newly dyed fabric billows in the sunshine. So many slippers and lamps and boxes and bags. So many people intent on selling their wares. I try to put them off politely with a little phrase in the local dialect - *blesh shokran* - thank you but it's not necessary. Mostly this works.

The airport is in the process of being made modern and swanky - all towering ceilings and glass and reflections. You have to wander through all the new construction to get to the old bit which resembles a French provincial railway station. However splendid the new one will be, I retain an affection for the old one. Roger, a childhood friend, arrives and I'm transformed again into amateur tour guide - a role I always relish however often I see the same sights.

The Majorelle Gardens, replete with gold fish and frog inhabited pools, surround the villa which is resplendently Majorelle blue which after the omnipresent corals and pinks is both jolting and wonderful. We get there very early before the cafe is properly open and are served hot chocolate. Cats lurk in the thick stands of bamboo stalking the many twittering birds.

The Badhi Palace is huge, a shadow really of its former self since the walls were stripped of their tiles so Moulay Ismail's Tomb in Meknes could be decorated with the spoils. The Bahdi always reminds me of Shelley's sonnet Ozymandias -*"Look on my work, ye mighty, and despair…"* Bare walls surround sunken gardens now filled with rose bushes and orange trees. Atop the walls are storks' nests.

Roger's visit coincides with with some sort of festival which entails much banging of brightly painted ceramic drums which are the delight of every young person in the medina. What is being celebrated exactly?

New Year's

Independence Day

The birthday of the prophet

A visit by the king of Jordan

All these are greeted with the happy sounds of drums and tambourines. Children ring the doorbell and knock on the door at all hours. *Un dirham! Un dirham!* I only give to the children I know well.

The drum beats reverberate off the walls of the narrow derb. They continue all evening and into the night. Young men congregate just outside our front door where there is a covered space.

At twelve thirty am I go out to plead with the young men and at first they think I'm pleased to see such a lovely celebration as they dance and sing and rock and drum.

Bonne fete! Happy holiday! Now, please would it be possible to be joyful a little further down the alley? My husband doesn't feel well. Roger comes out in his dressing-gown to help me. At last the celebrants reluctantly agree. Peace at last. I think there is only two more nights of it.

I decide to escape the drumming by taking Roger to Essouira. The Supratours bus stop is right next to the railway station where they let you photograph the red plastic CocaCola chairs in the waiting space but not the station itself. I hope the bus doesn't smash into anything this time.

We set off in bright sunshine but after Chichuoia a thick fog descends, a real pea-souper that envelops everything - you can see nothing at all out of the bus windows. It's the first fog I have ever encountered in Morocco. Cars have their headlights on. When we stopped for people to get a snack, you couldn't see the other side of the road.

Outside Essouira the fog lifts, the sun shines again and the seagulls circled the innards of fish by the docks where the bright blue fishing boats unload their cargo. The Atlantic waves smash against jagged rocks beyond the Portuguese ramparts and I think what a place for a ship wreck.

In Essouira there are gangs of short legged dogs who vie with the cats for their spoils. We think there must have been some sort of Alpha dog whose genes are replenished the population. Luckily the return trip to Marrakesh is uneventful.

To revert to the cat soap opera. We currently have Mimi, the main character, and her teenaged son Ollie who sleeps on our bed most of the day having spent the night out with his disreputable chums. Booger senior is confined to the roof because when he manages to break into the house he still sprays everywhere. Add Ginger - a sleek pretty orange and white large kitten - the cynosure of all eyes. Ollie, not quite knowing what to do yet, smacks her in a junior high sort of way. Old Booger lets Ginger share his food because he loves her, but she, of course, cannot be bothered with such a scruffy old man. And then there are the "Not-Ollies" a group of young cats who resemble Ollie. And Tufty who is large and tabby with extra hairy ears. We don't feed him but he sneaks up when we aren't looking.

In the derb there is a cousin of Mr. Booger's who hangs round the haunt waiting to be offered little triangles of Laughing Cow cheese which foolish people occasionally buy for him.

Poor Mimi's love life is at an end - the only cat in the medina who had been reduced to wearing one of those plastic collars after her operation. She hopes no one now remembers her humiliation.

Ashura, the drumming holiday, is now officially over. Several people have stopped us in the derb and asked if we are sleeping better and have been quite solicitous as to our health. I feel rather touched and guilty having suggested that my husband wasn't well. A few small boys whose drums have not yet broken still wander around giving the odd tap here and there, but on the whole peace reigns.

Roger's holiday was now drawing to an end and he needed to get all sorts of little presents to take back to friends in England. I love having people to stay - and quite look forward to them leaving. I think all of the potion sellers are quite used to people taking ages and ages to make the smallest of purchases. Roger is a world class ditherer and when I took him to a merchant I know near the Bahia Palace, I realized I was in for a long morning. We sat next to the stuffed alligator and were shown all sorts of ceramic or stone items for filing down the calluses on your feet, and little twig like things to act as toothpicks. We sipped mint tea and chatted as Roger amassed a collection of disparate items to haul home. Most of these things cost next to nothing but since we took up most of the seller's morning and presents had been bought for twelve people at least, I was not surprised that the total account came to something around fifty dollars. Actual value probably around twenty or less - but add in the entertainment value and the tea and the *petits cadeaux* and so on - I thought it a pretty fair price. Roger was delighted. The seller was also delighted and proceeded to load me up with even more *petits cadeaux* - rose scented soap and dried rose petals. These I handed on to Roger and he was even more thrilled with his morning's bargaining. I had forgotten that quite often tour guides get a kick back for bringing customers in. Backsheesh and rather charming. We all parted the best of friends.

27th January was Robert's birthday and we went out to the Barrage for a celebratory lunch over looking the water which is a little further out than usual since there has been a drought. Lunch consisted of salad and chicken and meat brochettes - and a huge pile of French fries - followed by sliced oranges sprinkled with cinnamon. A donkey wandered up to see what we were having - he liked the bread and oranges but rejected the orange peel. A few intrepid souls were swimming but I only managed to paddle.

February

We have lived in Morocco for almost two years without buying a single rug - a feat, I imagine few have managed since Marrakesh is a rug buyers' paradise - or hell depending on how you look at it. Most tourists get lured into cavernous warehouses, plied with mint tea and not allowed to escape until they have bought something.

The other day we were in Gueliz, not the medina at all, and passed a rather commonplace shop near the post office. There, hanging outside, was a black and white rug that could not have possibly been made by any machine known to man. It was ancient, grubby and threadbare in places…and just right for our house. Since we are lately almost suffering from color-fatigue we asked the salesman if we could look at other black and white rugs and were invited inside.

There were no other black and white rugs. He showed us two other rugs in glorious technicolor - obviously machine made. Then he went outside, pulled the black and white rug off the wall and presented it to us as the one masterpiece in the shop - which it was. He said it was made in the Middle Atlas.

We asked the price: 1,800 dirhams.

We offered 1,200.

He said 1,500 - the lowest he could possibly go. Special price since we were Marrakshi.

We said we'd come back - *ghedda, inshallah* - tomorrow, God willing.

He said 1,300 dirham.

Fine! Wrap it up.

Three rugs. No mint tea. The whole thing over in less than five minutes. Obviously we have not raised the art of carpet haggling to a very high level - but we do like the rug which has odd patches of red in it.

Door Knockers

Our lovely hand of Fatima door knocker has vanished. So have several others in the derb. We miss it, so replace it. The hand of Fatima is a sign of welcome. We think it very bad form to steal such things. Hmm…

Our pampered cats have become addicted to Whiskas - perfectly absurd in a country where most survive on scraps. In the middle of February the supply seemed to have run out. It was not to be had anywhere - not at Marjane or Acima nor even from the pet supplies place by the mellah. People are telephoning and emailing each other in search of Whiskas sightings. So the cats will have to get used to boiled up chicken bits with the bones taken out and should be grateful for them.

When walking between Ksour Agafy and Mouassine, I came upon a rather charming little shop selling hand embroidered items - pajamas and napkins and baby clothes all done on pure cotton and linen. I bought a lovely tablecloth with Berber designs. All these things are made by handicapped women in a workshop where childcare is provided. This is altogether a most worthwhile enterprise.

One day in May it started to rain torrentially - buckets and buckets of it. The courtyard drain couldn't cope and water rose several inches deep. The rain seeped in through cracks in the terrace and managed filter downwards to create a bulge in the hall ceiling so alarming that we took a broomstick and broke a hole in the plaster to let the water out before the whole ceiling caved in. The rain continued relentlessly. I retreated to our bedroom with my computer to try to do some writing.

Then there came an insistent ringing of the doorbell and loud knockings on the front door. Wretched kids with nothing to do, I thought and tried to ignore it. The knocking and tweeting continued. Finally I got up and opened the front door and a wall of filthy water cascaded over the stoop, through the hall and down the steps into the courtyard filling it to a depth of about eight inches. I shouted for Robert.

The flash flood had inundated the derb where the metal drain cover had been covered in plastic to minimize the stench but also prevented the water escaping. Robert went out and groped through the swirling muck and wrenched up the metal drain cover and removed the plastic and quite a lot of the water was sucked down into the sewer. But we were left with a perfectly filthy courtyard. We threw several bottles of bleach into the slop and started cleaning up. We should have worn gumboots had we had them - which we didn't - so worked in plastic flip flops. Luckily we escaped getting any vile diseases which was remarkable since who knows what donkey and cat poop and generally disgusting detritus was contained in the water. We had several showers each that day and replastered the hall roof a few days later when most of the damp had abated.

In the summer of 2008 we returned to America for all sorts of reasons - the most pressing of which was Robert's mother's increasing dementia. We didn't think it fair for Bobby to be her nearest relative. Robert was a long way from his gallery in Chelsea. We had a reasonable offer for the little house. A whole compendium of little things. We were incredibly sad to leave Ghislan and Ismail and all our friends and made promises to return - which we have done - often. We have even gone back to the little house which was so extensively refurbished - actually rebuilt - as to be another place entirely. Unbeknownst to us it was in danger of collapsing . So the little house has vanished and is now a fond memory often revisited in dreams and still longed for.

Afterword

Books

So much has been written about Morocco. Herewith some samples of the genre:

The very best is Peter Mayne's *A Year in Marrakesh* that I've often mentioned before. Even though it was written more than sixty years ago, so much is instantly recognizable. Mayne's cast of characters are vividly and amusingly described and he revels in their foibles. They include the caleche driver who insists that Mayne wants the roof up when he would much prefer to see the view as he is driven towards the medina from the station. Haroun, the dwarf, not in the least put out by his small stature, who thinks his height gives him an advantage - he can easily bite people's kneecaps. Abdlesem who wants to wear Mayne's tie for a party and uses the most roundabout means to achieve his aim. We spend part of each day in Cafe France in the northeast corner of the square where Mayne sat trying to write his novel amidst countless distractions.

In Mayne's day there weren't any mopeds - luckily - the streets were unpaved and water had to be collected from a communal tap. His accommodations were pretty primitive - though he does visit the exquisite Hotel Mamounia - now sadly closed for extensive refurbishment. An acute observer, Mayne presents a view of people he doesn't quite understand, but, like

Cafe France, so much remains unchanged - particularly the Marrakshi character.

Many of the people Mayne describes seem to have sprung directly from the pages of *A Thousand and One Nights* - that compendium of scheming viziers, astoundingly beautiful women, impoverished shoemakers, and amazing holes in the ground leading to untold treasure. The sorcerer in Aladdin and the Enchanted Lamp came from Morocco. He was "deeply versed in astrology, and could, by the power of his magic, uproot a mountain and hurl it against another." Obviously a pretty powerful fellow! Though many of the tales are set in Baghdad and Cairo, the world of wonders - of genii and hairbreadth escapes - are retold nightly in Djemma Elfna to rapt audiences. Even if you can't understand the words you are sure to get a waft of the miraculous, scurrilous and amazing. Those with a ribald sense of humor will relish The Historic Fart where an unfortunate merchant "was so mortified and filled with shame he wished the ground would open up and swallow him." When he returns to city after many years' exile he discovers this embarrassing episode has not been forgotten...

Those tempted to buy an enticing, dilapidated Moroccan palace or riad to restore will either be encouraged or put off by Tahir Shah's amusing and sometimes alarming account of his renovation of a huge haunted house in Casablanca. As you read *The Caliph's House* you feel glad that all the various disasters that befall him - including plagues of locusts, bees and giant mosquitos and workmen falling through roofs - didn't happen to you. Then you half wish you had the guts to undertake something so quixotic and wonderful. Like Peter Mayne and the writers of The Arabian nights, Shah delights in the mischievous, puzzling and sometimes maddening characters he encounters. After living in Morocco for only two years and attempting the most minor renovations and restorations, I ended up thinking that on the whole it's less hair-raising to read about it than actually do it.

The best known writer about North Africa is probably the legendary Paul Bowles. His most famous work, *The Sheltering Sky*, though set in Algeria, reveals both the attractions and dangers of a landscape and society quite 'other' than the west. It's beautifully written, sharply evocative of sights, sounds and smells but altogether a dark and unsettling read whose three main characters - Port a narcissistic dilettante, Kit, his equally drifting wife and their companion Tunner, have little to endear them to the reader. That two of them meet horrible fates is not much of a surprise.

Another very wonderful book - but very hard to get hold of - is *Women of Marrakesh* by Leonora Peets a Lithuanian doctor's wife who lived in Marrakesh between 1929 and 1970. A fascinating glimpse into the very cloistered world of Marrakshi women. Some very spooky stories here including the chilling Couscous of the Dead.

Printed in Great Britain
by Amazon